by
Eleanor Angeles

SCHOLASTIC
PROFESSIONAL **B**OOKS

New York • Toronto • London • Auckland • Sydney
Mexico City • New Delhi • Hong Kong • Buenos Aires

Photo credits:
Illustration credits:
Cover design by Solás
Interior design by Solás

ISBN: 0-439-23777-7
Copyright © 2002

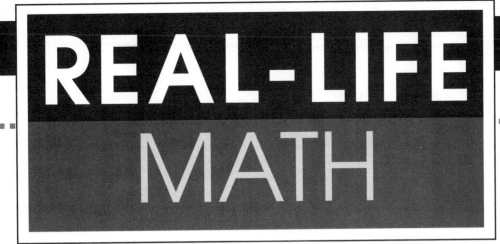

CONTENTS

Introduction **5**
   Before You Begin 6

Section 1: Just the Facts **7**
   1. Addition 8
   2. Subtraction 11
   3. Multiplication 13
   4. Division 16
   5. Estimating 19
   6. How to Use a Pocket Calculator 21
   7. Skills Survey 23

Section 2: Your Daily Math **24**
   1. Money Tracker 25
   2. (Unit Price x Quantity) + Sales Tax 26
   3. Paying for a Meal 27
   4. How to Save on Transportation 29
   5. At the Grocery 30
   6. In the Post Office 31
   7. Putting It All Together 32
   8. Skills Survey 33

Section 3: Your Money and Math **34**
   1. Checking Account 35
   2. Balancing Your Checkbook 37
   3. Savings 39
   4. Budgeting 41
   5. Renting an Apartment 43
   6. Are You Covered? 45
   7. All About Credit 46
   8. Filing Your Income Tax 48
   9. Putting It All Together 50
   10. Skills Survey 52

Section 4: Math Goes to Work **53**
   1. The Best Paying Job 54
   2. Working Time 55
   3. Time-and-a-Half 56
   4. Earning by the Piece or by Commission 58
   5. What Is Profit? Loss? 59
   6. Pricing 61
   7. Bookkeeping 62
   8. Putting It All Together 63
   9. Skills Survey 65

Section 5: Math Savers **66**
   1. City and Highway Mileage 67
   2. Gas Saving Habits 69
   3. Do It Yourself 70
   4. Using the Calculator's Memory 71
   5. Discounts 73
   6. Buy More, Pay Less 74
   7. Putting It All Together 75
   8. Skills Survey 76

Section 6: Math Where You Least Expect It 77
   1. Where Does Your Team Stand? 78
   2. Going Places 79
   3. Temperature Change 81
   4. The Metric System 83
   5. Shopping With Foreign Money 85
   6. Putting It All Together 87
   7. Skills Survey 88

Glossary **89**
   Answer Key 91

WHO NEEDS SCHOLASTIC REAL-LIFE MATH?

You do.

Because no matter what you do in life, **math is there.**

Scholastic Real-Life Math gives you practice using math for everyday situations.

To get and keep a job, you need math skills.

To run a home or a workshop, you need math skills.

In sports, travel, shopping—you use math every day.

So, whether you need math at the grocery store or on a vacation, each section will improve your necessary math skills.

Most lessons have a **Quick Reference Box.** This is the information you will need to do the exercises.

If you need help with any of the calculations, just turn to page 89. Here, in the **Glossary,** you will find the meanings of any unfamiliar words. Remember to keep a pad of paper by you at all times: You will need it for calculations!

The **Skills Survey** pages at the end of each section can be used to test your progress.

Here is some basic information you will need to know before going any further.

Place Values

The value of 5 in each of the places shown on the chart is different. Each place has ten times the value of the next place to the right. A 5 in the hundreds place has a value of 5 x 100, or 500. A 5 in the hundredths place has a value of $5 \times \frac{1}{100}$, or $\frac{5}{100}$. Another way to represent $\frac{5}{100}$ is .05.

PLACE VALUES

Billions	Hundred Millions	Ten Millions	Millions	Hundred Thousands	Ten Thousands	Thousands	Hundreds	Tens	Ones	.	Tenths	Hundredths	Thousandths
5,	5	5	5,	5	5	5,	5	5	5	.	5	5	5

Answer the following questions.

1. What is the value of 2 in the hundreds place? _____

2. What is the value of 2 in the hundredths place? _____

3. 3/10 is another way to represent 3 in the _____ place.

4. An 8 in the thousands place has a value of _____.

5. .008 means that the 8 is in the _____ place.

Write the following numerals in the Place Values Chart at right. The first one is done for you.

PLACE VALUES

	Billions	Hundred Millions	Ten Millions	Millions	Hundred Thousands	Ten Thousands	Thousands	Hundreds	Tens	Ones	.	Tenths	Hundredths	Thousandths
Thirteen million, one hundred thirty-four thousand, nine hundred twenty			1	3,	1	3	4,	9	2	0	.	0	0	0
Seventy eight and two tenths														
Six hundred fifty-five thousand, two hundred seventeen														
Two hundred thirty-four														
One billion, five hundred six million, and one hundred twenty-five thousand														
Eight thousand two hundred twenty-one and five hundredths														

section 1

You are a mathematician.

When you're **buying** groceries, **counting** change, or **scoring** a ballgame, you are using **math skills**.

The exercises in Section 1 will help you prepare for the real-life problems you will face later on in this book.

Contents

1. Addition 8

2. Subtraction 11

3. Multiplication 13

4. Division 16

5. Estimating 19

6. How to Use a Pocket Calculator 21

   Skills Survey 23

1. ADDITION

Addition and Subtraction Table

Use this table to add and subtract. To add two numerals, find one in bold in the top row, and the other in bold in the left-hand column. To find your answer, follow their corresponding row and column until they meet. To subtract, work backward using the same method.

	0	1	2	3	4	5	6	7	8	9	10
0	0	1	2	3	4	5	6	7	8	9	10
1	1	2	3	4	5	6	7	8	9	10	11
2	2	3	4	5	6	7	8	9	10	11	12
3	3	4	5	6	7	8	9	10	11	12	13
4	4	5	6	7	8	9	10	11	12	13	14
5	5	6	7	8	9	10	11	12	13	14	15
6	6	7	8	9	10	11	12	13	14	15	16
7	7	8	9	10	11	12	13	14	15	16	17
8	8	9	10	11	12	13	14	15	16	17	18
9	9	10	11	12	13	14	15	16	17	18	19
10	10	11	12	13	14	15	16	17	18	19	20

Use the directions above to find the answers to the following problems. Write the letter of the problem next to each answer in the table.

      A. 13 − 6   B. 8 + 7   C. 14 − 9

We use addition to find out the **total** when we combine two or more numbers.

Complete the table below.

0 +0 0	0 +1 1	0 +2 2		0 +4 4	0 +5 5		0 +7 7	0 +8 8	0 +9 9
1 +0 1	1 +1 2	1 +2 3	1 +3 4			1 +6 7	1 +7 8	1 +8 9	1 +9 10
2 +0 2			2 +3 5	2 +4 6	2 +5 7	2 +6 8	2 +7 9	2 +8 10	2 +9 11
3 +1 4	3 +2 5		3 +4 7	3 +5 8	3 +6 9	3 +7 10	3 +8 11	3 +9 12	
4 +0 4	4 +1 5	4 +2 6	4 +3 7	4 +4 8		4 +6 10		4 +8 12	
5 +0 5	5 +1 6		5 +3 8		5 +5 10		5 +7 12	5 +8 13	5 +9 14
6 +0 6		6 +2 8		6 +4 10	6 +5 11	6 +6 12	6 +7 13	6 +8 14	
	7 +1 8	7 +2 9	7 +3 10		7 +5 12	7 +6 13	7 +7 14		7 +9 16
8 +0 8		8 +2 10		8 +4 12	8 +5 13	8 +6 14		8 +8 16	8 +9 17
9 +0 9	9 +1 10		9 +3 12	9 +4 13	9 +5 14		9 +7 16	9 +8 17	9 +9 18

Due to space limitations, these answers do not appear in the answer key.

Addition: Working Right to Left

When you add numbers with many digits, begin with the column on the right, the ones.

345

Hundreds	3	300
Tens	4	40
Ones	5	5

First add the ones:

    1.   **2.**   **3.**

301   a. 125   a. 617   a. 223

452   243   321   132

  3

Next, add the tens.

301   b. 125   b. 617   b. 223

452   243   321   132

  5

Then add the hundreds.

301   c. 125   c. 617   c. 223

452   243   321   132

  7

Write the sums.

753   4.   5.   6.

Addition: Working With More Than Two Numbers

Example: Find the sum of 5 + 3 + 9. First add 5 + 3 to get 8. Then add 9 to 8 to get 17. (Hint: When adding with more than two "addends," or numbers, you can group them first and add as you go along to make things easier.)

1. 2 + 1 + 5 = ___ + ___ =   _____
2. 3 + 4 + 6 = ___ + ___ =   _____
3. 4 + 5 + 2 + 1 = ___ + ___ =   _____
4. 1 + 3 + 7 + 9 = ___ + ___ =   _____
5. 6 + 5 + 8 + 7 = ___ + ___ =   _____

Addition: Regrouping

Example: Add 68 + 26. First, line up the two numbers to add them. Next, add the ones: 8 + 6 = 14. Write 4 beneath the ones column. You still have 1 ten from 14. Then add that 1 ten from 14 to the tens column. Add the tens: 1 + 6 + 2 = 9. Write 9 beneath the tens column. Your answer is 94.

```
      68                1
     +26               68
     ----             +26
      4                ----
                        94
```

Find the sums.

1. 74 +16	2. 57 +38	3. 26 +55	4. 49 +48
5. 78 +36	6. 85 +75	7. 49 +68	8. 39 +84
9. 175 +28	10. 29 +384	11. 354 +296	12. 158 +493
13. 126 +59	14. 782 +156	15. 365 +809	16. 485 +760
17. 924 +76	18. 864 + 247	19. 346 +876	20. 984 +249
21. 1787 +907	22. 2528 + 645	23. 2637 +7363	24. 1743 +9878

Lining Up Numbers to Add

Line up numbers by place value. Ones must line up with ones, tens must line up with tens, and so on. To add 23 + 1 + 3251 + 401, line them up this way:

```
  23
   1
3251
 401
```

Line up these addends and find the sums.

1. 235 + 4 + 61 + 4000 =

2. 4312 + 34 + 5 + 789 =

Adding Long Columns

You can add long columns of numbers in different ways. Here are some suggestions to solve the following problems.

Add the ones 5 + 8 + 4 + 2 = 19
Add the tens 50 + 50 + 30 + 10 = 140
Add the hundreds 400 + 600 + 800 + 200 = 2000

Then, add the ones, tens, and hundreds together.

```
 455          19
 658         140
 834       +2000
+212        2159
```

Or, try this method.

1. Add the first two numbers: 455 + 658 = 1113
2. Add the next two numbers: 834 + 212 = 1046

Then, add your two answers together to find the final sum (2159).

Find the sums using the method that's easiest for you.

1. 124 953 687 + 456	2. 875 235 492 + 618	3. 267 725 128 + 953	4. 786 935 547 109 + 63

Checking Sums

One way to check your answer in addition is to change the order of the "addends," or numbers you're adding. You should always get the same sum. Practice this by checking your answers for questions 1– 4, above.

Example:

```
 439          861
 861          614
 123          439
 614          123
2037         2037
```

Subtraction of Whole Numbers

We use subtraction to find the **difference** between two numbers.

Complete the table below.

0 −0 0	1 −0 1	2 −0 2		4 −0 4	5 −0 5	6 −0 6		8 −0 8	9 −0 9	
1 −1 0	2 −1 1		4 −1 3	5 −1 4	6 −1 5		8 −1 7		10 −1 9	
2 −2 0		4 −2 2	5 −2 3	6 −2 4		8 −2 6	9 −2 7	10 −2 8		
	4 −3 1	5 −3 2	6 −3 3	7 −3 4	8 −3 5		10 −3 7		12 −3 9	
4 −4 0	5 −4 1	6 −4 2	7 −4 3		9 −4 5	10 −4 6		12 −4 8	13 −4 9	
5 −5 0	6 −5 1		8 −5 3	9 −5 4		11 −5 6	12 −5 7	13 −5 8	14 −5 9	
6 −6 0		8 −6 2		10 −6 4	11 −6 5		13 −6 7	14 −6 8	15 −6 9	
	8 −7 1	9 −7 2	10 −7 3		12 −7 5	13 −7 6		15 −7 8	16 −7 9	
8 −8 0		10 −8 2		12 −8 4	13 −8 5	14 −8 6	15 −8 7		17 −8 9	
9 −9 0	10 −9 1		12 −9 3	13 −9 4	14 −9 5	15 −9 6	16 −9 7	17 −9 8		

Due to space limitations, these answers do not appear in the answer key.

The Relationship Between Addition and Subtraction

Addition		Subtraction
2	?	5
+3	+3	−3
5	5	2 — difference

Find the Differnece

Rewrite each addition problem below as a subtraction problem. Then find the difference.

1. ? **2.** 22   **3.** ?
   $+\,9$ $+\,?$
   18   28   39

4. 35   **5.** ?   **6.** 701
   $+?$ $+213$ $+\,?$
   347   635   705

Renaming and Regrouping

Example: Subtract 45 – 18.

First, rewrite 45 as 3 tens and 15 ones.
Place the 15 ones in the ones column and the 3 in the tens column.

$$\begin{array}{r} 3\ 15 \\ \cancel{45} \\ -18 \\ \hline \end{array}$$

Then subtract the ones.
$$15 - 8 = 7.$$

Write 7 beneath the ones column.
Finally, subtract the tens.

$$\begin{array}{r} 3\ 15 \\ \cancel{45} \\ -18 \\ \hline 27 \end{array}$$

In each example below, the larger number can be renamed before the smaller number is subtracted. Find the differences.

$$\begin{array}{r} 2\ 14 \\ \cancel{34} \\ -\ 6 \\ \hline 28 \end{array}$$

1. 22 **2.** 35 **3.** 26 **4.** 47 **5.** 58
  $-\,6$ $-\,3$ $-\,8$ $-\,7$ $-\,9$ $-\,9$

$$\begin{array}{r} 4\ 11\ 15 \\ \cancel{525} \\ -\ 86 \\ \hline 439 \end{array}$$

6. 431 **7.** 352 **8.** 234 **9.** 655 **10.** 286
  $-\,86$ $-\,63$ $-\,74$ $-\,55$ $-\,66$ $-\,98$

$$\begin{array}{r} 7\ 14\ 13 \\ \cancel{853} \\ -787 \\ \hline 66 \end{array}$$

11. 222 **12.** 425 **13.** 512 **14.** 356 **15.** 685
  -787 $-\,169$ $-\,358$ $-\,424$ $-\,267$ $-\,598$

$$\begin{array}{r} 3\ 9\ 9\ 10 \\ \cancel{4000} \\ -287 \\ \hline 3713 \end{array}$$

16. 300 **17.** 5200 **18.** 2005 **19.** 1050 **20.** 3020
  -287 $-\,23$ $-\,199$ $-\,576$ $-\,561$ $-\,342$

Checking the Difference

One way of checking your answer to a subtraction problem is to add the difference and the smaller number. The sum should be equal to the larger number. Practice this by checking your answers to 1–20 above.

$$\begin{array}{rcl} 1260 & & 1073 \\ -\ 187 & \longrightarrow & +\ 187 \\ \hline 1073 & & 1260 \end{array}$$

To find the cost of 5 shirts at $6 each, you can add 6 + 6 + 6 + 6 + 6. A quicker way is to multiply.

Multiplication and Division Table

	1	2	3	4	5	6	7	8	9	10
0	0	0	0	0	0	0	0	0	0	0
1	1	2	3	4	5	6	7	8	9	10
2	2	4	6	8	10	12	14	16	18	20
3	3	6	9	12	15	18	21	24	27	30
4	4	8	12	16	20	24	28	32	36	40
5	5	10	15	20	25	30	35	40	45	50
6	6	12	18	24	30	36	42	48	54	60
7	7	14	21	28	35	42	49	56	63	70
8	8	16	24	32	40	48	56	64	72	80
9	9	18	27	36	45	54	63	72	81	90
10	10	20	30	40	50	60	70	80	90	100

Use this table to multiply and divide. To multiply two numerals, find one in bold in the top row, and the other in bold in the left-hand column. To find your answer, follow their corresponding row and column until they meet. To divide, work backward using the same method. The answers to the following problems can be found in the table. Write the letter of the problem next to each answer in the table above.   A. 36 ÷ 9   B. 7 x 9   C. 42 ÷ 6

Multiplication of Whole Numbers

Complete the table below.

0 x 0 0	1 x 0 0	2 x 0 0	3 x 0 0	4 x 0 0		6 x 0 0	7 x 0 0	8 x 0 0	9 x 0 0
	1 x 1 1	2 x 1 2	3 x 1 3	4 x 1 4	5 x 1 5		7 x 1 7	8 x 1 8	9 x 1 9
0 x 2 0		2 x 2 4	3 x 2 6	4 x 2 8	5 x 2 10	6 x 2 12		8 x 2 16	9 x 2 18
0 x 3 0	1 x 3 3		3 x 3 9	4 x 3 12	5 x 3 15	6 x 3 18	7 x 3 21		9 x 3 27
0 x 4 0	1 x 4 4	2 x 4 8		4 x 4 16	5 x 4 20	6 x 4 24	7 x 4 28	8 x 4 32	
0 x 5 0	1 x 5 5	2 x 5 10	3 x 5 15		5 x 5 25	6 x 5 30	7 x 5 35		9 x 5 45
0 x 6 0	1 x 6 6	2 x 6 12		4 x 6 24	5 x 6 30	6 x 6 36		8 x 6 48	9 x 6 54
0 x 7 0	1 x 7 7		3 x 7 21	4 x 7 28	5 x 7 35		7 x 7 49	8 x 7 56	9 x 7 63
0 x 8 0		2 x 8 16	3 x 8 24	4 x 8 32		6 x 8 48	7 x 8 56	8 x 8 64	9 x 8 72
0 x 9 0		2 x 9 18	3 x 9 27		5 x 9 45	6 x 9 54	7 x 9 63	8 x 9 72	9 x 9 81

Due to space limitations, these answers do not appear in the answer key.

Multiplication: Working From Right to Left

Example: Multiply 123 x 2.

First, multiply 3 x 2 to get 6. Write 6.

Then multiply 2 x 2 to get 4. Write 4   123
to the left of 6.   x 2
Finally, multiply 1 x 2 to get 2.   246
Write 2 to the left of 4.

Your final answer is called a "product."

Find the products.

1. 23	**2.** 385	**3.** 301	**4.** 72
x 3	x 1	x 2	x 4
5. 80	**6.** 511	**7.** 802	**8.** 931
x 7	x 6	x 4	x 3

Using Your Memory in Multiplication

Example: Multiply 87 x 4.

First, multiply 7 x 4 to get 28.   87
                                                        x 4
Write 8.   8

Remember the 2 to get from 28. Then
multiply 8 x 4 to get 32. Add the 2 from   87
the previous step. 32 + 2 = 34.   x4
For the final answer, write 34 to the   348
left of 8.

Find the products.

1. 95	**2.** 87	**3.** 64
x 6	x 5	x 8
4. 137	**5.** 209	**6.** 514
x 2	x 4	x 7

Using Two Partial Products

To find 27 x 56, you can use the following method.

```
      27
    x 56
     162 (27 x 6) partial product
   +1350 (27 x 50) partial product
    1512 (162 + 1350) PRODUCT
```

Note: You do not have to write the 0 in 1350,
because you will get the same product whether you
write it or not.

Find the products.

1. 42	**2.** 46	**3.** 81
x 23	x 31	x 19
4. 132	**5.** 345	**6.** 1213
x 24	x 63	x 32

Using Three Partial Products

To find the product of 692 x 231, you can use the
following method.

```
       692
     x 231
       692   (692 x 1) partial product
     20760   (692 x 30) partial product
   +138400   (692 x 200) partial product
    159852   PRODUCT
```

Find the products.

1. 765	**2.** 348	**3.** 879	**4.** 647
x 211	x 123	x 312	x 251

Zeros in Multiplication

Your solution to 225 x 304 may be found in different ways. Here are some suggestions.

First method:

```
      225
    x 304
      900
      000  (include the partial
    +675  product of zero)
    68400
```

Second method:

```
      225
    x 304
      900
      675  (leave out the zero)
    68400
```

Use either method to find the products.

1. 352	**2.** 864	**3.** 506	**4.** 708
x 205	x 302	x 201	x 403

Multiplying by 10, 100, 1000

To multiply a number by 10, 100, or 1000, here's what you do.

35 x 10 = 350

(35 x 1, add 1 zero)

35 x 100 = 3500

(35 x 1, add 2 zeros)

35 x 1000 = 35000

(35 x 1, add 3 zeros)

Find the products.

1. 58 x 10 = _____

2. 58 x 100 = _____

3. 58 x 1000 = _____

4. 60 x 100 = _____

5. 45 x 10 = _____

6. 99 x 1000 = _____

7. 125 x 100 = _____

Checking Your Answers

One way of checking your answer to a multiplication problem is to interchange the two numbers to be multiplied. Practice this by checking your answers on this page.

```
                        Check:
      43                   15
    x 15                 x 43
     215                  415
     430                  600
     645 ◄── PRODUCT ──► 645
```

4. Division

Division of Whole Numbers

How can you find the price of 1 book if 5 books cost $20? You can **divide**.

Complete the table below.

0 1)0	1 1)1	2 1)2	3 1)3		5 1)5		7 1)7	8 1)8	9 1)9
0 2)0	1 2)2	2 2)4		4 2)8	5 2)10	6 2)12		8 2)16	9 2)18
0 3)0	1 3)3		3 3)9	4 3)12	5 3)15	6 3)18	7 3)21		9 3)27
0 4)0		2 4)8	3 4)12	4 4)16	5 4)20	6 4)24	7 4)28	8 4)32	
	1 5)5	2 5)10	3 5)15	4 5)20		6 5)30	7 5)35		9 5)45
0 6)0		2 6)12	3 6)18	4 6)24	5 6)30	6 6)36		8 6)48	9 6)54
0 7)0	1 7)7		3 7)21	4 7)28	5 7)35		7 7)49	8 7)56	9 7)63
0 8)0	1 8)1	2 8)16		4 8)32		6 8)48	7 8)56	8 8)64	9 8)72
0 9)0	1 9)9	2 9)18	3 9)27		5 9)45	6 9)54	7 9)63	8 9)72	

Due to space limitations, these answers do not appear in the answer key.

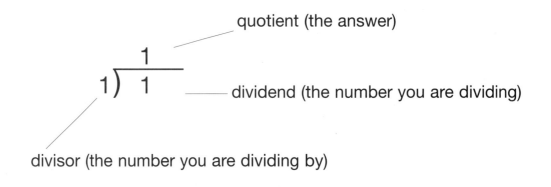

quotient (the answer)

dividend (the number you are dividing)

divisor (the number you are dividing by)

Here is an easy, step-by-step guide to finding a quotient.

Divide: $96\overline{)4608}$

To begin, 96 does not go into 4 or 46. So, how many 96's are in 460? Estimate by finding how many 9's are in 46. 46 ÷ 9 is about 5, so try 5.

$$\begin{array}{r} 5 \\ 96\overline{)4608} \\ -480 \end{array}$$

But 96 x 5 is 480. You can't subtract because the answer is still too big. Now try 4. 96 x 4 is 384, which can be subtracted from 460. Bring down the 8 from the dividend. Now, how many 96's are in 768? Estimate by finding how many 9's are in 76. 76 ÷ 9 is about 8, so try 8.

$$\begin{array}{r} 48 \\ 96\overline{)4608} \\ 384 \\ 768 \end{array}$$

Try 4.
384 can be subtracted from 460.
Bring down the 8.
Now, how many 96's are in 768?

Remember: You can check if your answer is reasonable by estimating. 96 is about 100 and 48 is about 50. 100 x 50 = 5000. 4608 is about 5000, so the answer is reasonable.

Solving Division Problems

276 ÷ 23 is usually solved this way.

$$\begin{array}{r} 12 \\ 23\overline{)276} \\ -23 \\ \hline 46 \\ -46 \\ \hline 00 \end{array}$$

(1 x 23)
(2 x 23)

Find the quotients.

1. $9\overline{)828}$ **2.** $18\overline{)234}$

Zeros in the Quotient

The answer to 2461 ÷ 23 might be incorrectly written as 17. It should be 107. To avoid this error, you may write your work like this.

$$\begin{array}{r} 107 \\ 23\overline{)2461} \\ -23 \\ \hline 16 \\ -00 \\ \hline 161 \\ -161 \\ \hline 000 \end{array}$$ quotient

Remember: Each time you bring down one digit from the dividend, you must write one digit in the quotient.

You may also avoid mistakes by estimating or "guessing" the quotient to check your work. For example:

Estimate 2461 ÷ 23.

Round 2461 to 2000 and 23 to 20.

Since 2000 ÷ 20 = 100, you know that the quotient is about 100. So 17 is wrong.

Find the quotients.

1. $32\overline{)6592}$ **2.** $19\overline{)5795}$

3. $24\overline{)9696}$ **4.** $17\overline{)8534}$

17

Short Method of Dividing Rounded Numbers

To multiply 200 x 20, you simply write three zeros and multiply 2 x 2. Your answer is 4000.

To divide 4000 ÷ 200, this is what you do:

$4000 ÷ 200 = 40 ÷ 2 = 20$

To divide 8000 ÷ 4000:

$8000 ÷ 4000 = 8 ÷ 4 = 2$

Based on these examples, here is a simple rule for dividing rounded numbers: Cross off the same number of zeros from the divisor and dividend and divide the numbers you are left with.

Find the quotients.

1. $6000 ÷ 2000 = $ _____
2. $4500 ÷ 900 = $ _____
3. $3500 ÷ 700 = $ _____
4. $800 ÷ 200 = $ _____

What will be the first digit in each quotient?

1. a. $40\overline{)1728}$ b. $48\overline{)1728}$

2. a. $70\overline{)3672}$ b. $72\overline{)3672}$

3. a. $20\overline{)1152}$ b. $24\overline{)1152}$

Using Remainders in Division

Here's a practical example of how remainders in division affect your everyday life: telling time.

To change minutes to hours, you divide the number of minutes by 60. (60 min. = 1 hr.) Sometimes there are leftover minutes. In division, these leftovers are called remainders. Take a look at the following example.

135 min. ÷ 60 min. = ?

The answer is 2 hours and 15 minutes.

$$\begin{array}{r} 2 \\ 60\overline{)135} \\ \underline{120} \\ 15 \end{array} \text{ (remainder)}$$

You will not only find this useful with time, but with other measurements as well.

Find the quotients and the remainders.

1. 198 min. ÷ 60 min. = ...hours ......minutes

2. 56 inches ÷ 12 inches = ...feet ....inches

3. 86 days ÷ 24 hours = ...days ....hours

4. 556 ounces ÷ 16 ounces = ...pounds ....ounces

"Guessing" the Answer

How often do you ask yourself, "Do I have enough money?" You can find a quick, reasonable answer by estimating, or "guessing" to find a close answer to a math problem.

> **Quick Reference**
>
> The question to be answered often tells you how to estimate. For example, here are two different questions about the same advertisement. The estimates are done in different ways. What is the cost of 2 batteries at 78¢ each?
>
> **Step 1:** Round 78¢ to 80¢
>
> **Step 2:** 80 + 80 or 80 x 2 is 160.
>
> So, the cost of 2 batteries is about $1.60
>
> OR
>
> Is $1.60 enough to buy 2 batteries?
>
> **Step 1:** Figure $1.60 ÷ 2 = 80¢
>
> **Step 2:** Since 78¢ is about 80¢, the answer is probably yes.

You may have your own ways of estimating. Here's a chance for you to use them. Look at the facts in the ad for cassettes below. Quickly guess the answer to each question and circle it. Do not use pencil and paper to find the answer.

1. How much does each cassette cost?

   About $1   About $2

2. Can you buy 2 cassettes for $4?

   Yes   No

3. How many cassettes can $12 buy?

   6   7   8

Guessing the answer to a problem is one way to check if your actual answer is right or wrong. For example, if your estimated answer is 1000 and your actual answer is 110, you know that you made a mistake somewhere. You should do the problem again.

There are many ways to estimate. As you've seen in previous sections, one common method used to estimate answers in math problems is to round numbers to the nearest ten, hundred, or thousand so that you can work with them more easily.

For example: Estimate 898 + 204

	898	is rounded to	900	
	+204	is rounded to	+200	
Sum	1102		1100	Estimate

Estimate the sums.

1. 813 + 692: _____ + _____ = _____

2. 3185 + 1812: _____ + _____ = _____

3. 62 + 78 + 39: _____ + _____ + _____ = _____

Estimate the differences.

1. 706 – 598: _____ – _____ = _____

2. 497 – 208: _____ – _____ = _____

3. 6028 – 3982: _____ – _____ = _____

Estimate the products.

1. 29 x 31: _____ x _____ = _____

2. 88 x 52: _____ x _____ = _____

3. 394 x 203 _____ x _____ = _____

Estimate the quotients.

1. 4105 ÷ 79: _____ ÷ _____ = _____

2. 2950 ÷ 51: _____ ÷ _____ = _____

6. How to Use a Pocket Calculator

A **pocket calculator** can save you a lot of time in solving math problems. Of course, you must tell it what you want it to do. This lesson will help you get more out of your calculator.

Some calculators have different features. The one shown here is a common type of calculator with a memory. The keys must be pressed in the correct order to get the right answer.

Here is an example that shows you how to use your calculator.

To add 12 + 35:

      A. Press AC (or C) to clear the machine.

        B. Press 1 and then 2 for 12. The read-out will show 12.

          C. You want to add, so press +.

            D. Press 3 and then 5 for 35. The read-out will show 35.

              E. Press = to get the answer. The read-out will show 47.

Now do this: 27 + 45 − 39

Press the keys in this order:

        AC 27+45 − 39 =

The read-out will show 33.

Use what you've learned.

1. To find the answer to 35 + 8, which is the correct order for pressing the keys?

a. AC 35 + 8 =

b. AC 358 + =

c. 35 AC + 8 =

d. 35 + AC = 8

2. To find the answer to 17 + 23 – 8, which is the correct order?

a. 17 + AC 238 – =

b. AC 17 + 23 – 8 =

c. 1 + 723 – AC = 8

d. AC 1723 + – 8 =

3. To find the answer to 7 x 8 + 4, which is the correct order?

a. AC 78 x + 4 =

b. 784 x + AC =

c. 7 x AC 8 = + 4

d. AC 7 x 8 + 4 =

4. Choose the correct operation (+, –, x, or ÷) and write it in the space provided.

a. 3 _____ 5 = 8

b. 13 _____ 6 = 7

c. 4 _____ 5 = 20

d. 18 _____ 3 = 6

5. Fill in the keys you must press to find the answer to each problem. The first one is done for you.

a. 31 + 23   AC 31 + 23 = _____

b. 17 – 11   _____

c. 49 ÷ 7   _____

d. 36 x 12   _____

e. 3 + 7 + 9 – 8   _____

f. 17 – 6 + 11 – 2   _____

To build on these calculator skills, please turn to page 71, Using the Calculator's Memory.

22

You have learned some essential math skills to help with your daily activities. The exercises in this section will help sharpen your skills.

Solve the math problems below without using a calculator.

1. 56
   +41

2. 352
   +26

3. 263
   +715

4. 2136
   +4041

5. 35
   + 6

6. 48
   + 25

7. 507
   +197

8. 726
   +384

Line up the addends and find the sums without using a calculator.

9. 42 + 200 + 2312 + 3 =

10. 4 + 7201 + 33 + 120 =

Subtract without using a calculator.

11. 48
   −17

12. 352
   −85

13. 6000
   −134

14. 3060
   −483

Multiply without using a calculator.

15. 32
   x 3

16. 602
   x 2

17. 75
   x4

18. 412
   x7

19. 24
   x32

20. 253
   x26

21. 531
   x213

22. 304
   x502

Divide without using a calculator.

23. 32)384

24. 8)776

25. 26)7904

26. 4500 ÷ 90 =

Your Daily Math

section 2

Where has all the money gone? How much do I have to **save** to **buy** that car? How can I **earn** more? Which item is the better buy? What's the score?

You can now **use your math skills** to answer these questions, and more.

Contents

1. Money Tracker 25

2. (Unit Price x Quantity) + Sales Tax 26

3. Paying for a Meal 27

4. How to Save on Transportation 29

5. At the Grocery 30

6. In the Post Office 31

7. Putting It All Together 32

   Skills Survey 33

This lesson answers the question, **"Where has all the money gone?"** and will help you keep track of your expenses.

Quick Reference

Balance is the cash or money on hand.

When subtracting money, be sure that the decimal points are lined up.

The **difference**, or **new balance**, is the answer to a subtraction problem.

To check each answer, add the difference and the amount subtracted. The sum should be the same as the original amount. For example:

$150.00	$148.50
−1.50	+1.50
$148.50	$150.00

Complete this week's calendar of expenses. Subtract the expense, or amount paid, from each balance. Write your answers on the lines provided. Make sure to carry over each End-of-Day balance to the start of the next day.

Keep track of your Saturday expenses. Write the amount of money you have on the first line. Subtract each expense. How much do you have at the end of the day?

EXPENSE CALENDAR

	Sunday	Monday	Tuesday	Wednesday	Thursday	Friday	Saturday
Start-of-Day Balance	$350.00	$328.78					
Expense	Bus Fare 1.50	Train Ticket 10.00	Photo Developing 7.02	Sweater 16.99	Groceries 11.83	Newspapers 1.20	
New Balance	348.50						
Expense	Contribution 5.00	Breakfast 3.39	Film 4.83	Jeans 32.98	Legal Pad 1.67	Birthday Gift 9.87	
New Balance	343.50						
Expense	Laundry 3.60	CDs 11.74	Lunch 5.68	T-shirt 10.27	Notebook 1.74	Flowers 3.25	
New Balance	339.90						
Expense	Newspaper .75	Band Aids 4.08	Light Bulbs 2.70	Running Shoes 58.36	Pen 1.37	Plant 4.99	
New Balance	339.15						
Expense	Ball Game 2.50	Watch Repair 15.63	Picture Frame 3.79	Snack 2.27	Paperback 3.08	Vase 6.25	
New Balance	332.65						
Expense	Snack 1.87	Magazine 2.25	Socks 4.32	Exercise Class 10.00		Concert Tickets 37.00	
New Balance	328.78						
Expense			Dry Cleaners 8.10			Cab Fare 6.35	
New Balance							
Expense						Dinner 12.90	
End-of-Day Balance	328.78						

Due to space limitations, these answers do not appear in the answer key.

Have you ever been surprised that the bill for a $10.00 item is $10.60? This lesson will help you understand **sales tax** and how it affects the amount a customer pays.

On each **sales receipt**, find the total cost of the items described by **multiplying** the unit by the price quantity. Then add the amounts in the total-cost column to find the subtotal. Use the sales tax chart to

6% Sales Tax Chart

Amount of Sale	Tax	Amount of Sale	Tax	Amount of Sale	Tax	Amount of Sale	Tax
$.00 – .10	none	2.51 – 2.67	.16	5.18 – 5.34	.32	7.68 – 7.84	.47
.11 – .17	.01	2.68 – 2.84	.17	5.35 – 5.50	.33	7.85 – 8.10	.48
.18 – .34	.02	2.85 – 3.10	.18	5.51 – 5.67	.34	8.11 – 8.17	.49
.35 – .50	.03	3.11 – 3.17	.19	5.68 – 5.84	.35	8.18 – 8.34	.50
.51 – .67	.04	3.18 – 3.34	.20	5.85 – 6.10	.36	8.35 – 8.50	.51
.68 – .84	.05	3.35 – 3.50	.21	6.11 – 6.17	.38	8.51 – 8.67	.52
.85 – 1.10	.06	3.51 – 3.67	.22	6.18 – 6.34	.39	8.68 – 8.84	.53
1.11 – 1.17	.07	3.68 – 3.84	.23	6.35 – 6.50	.40	8.85 – 9.10	.54
1.18 – 1.34	.08	3.85 – 4.10	.24	6.51 – 6.67	.41	9.11 – 9.17	.55
1.35 – 1.50	.09	4.11 – 4.17	.25	6.68 – 6.84	.42	9.18 – 9.34	.56
1.51 – 1.67	.10	4.18 – 4.34	.26	6.85 – 7.10	.42	9.35 – 9.50	.57
1.68 – 1.84	.11	4.35 – 4.50	.27	7.11 – 7.17	.43	9.51 – 9.67	.58
1.85 – 2.10	.12	4.51 – 4.67	.28	7.18 – 7.34	.44	9.68 – 9.84	.59
2.11 – 2.17	.13	4.68 – 4.84	.29	7.35 – 7.50	.45	9.85 – 10.00	.60
2.18 – 2.34	.14	4.85 – 5.10	.30	7.51 – 7.67	.46		
2.35 – 2.50	.15	5.11 – 5.17	.31				

determine the tax on the subtotal. Add the subtotal and the tax to find the final amount due from the customer. We did the first one for you.

sum of the amounts in total-cost column

Stationery

Item Description	Unit Price	Qty.	Total Cost
PENS	.79	3	$2.37
MEMO PAD	.39	5	1.95
SCOTCH TAPE	.41	1	.41
PENCILS	.15	4	.60
		Subtotal	$5.33
		6% Sales Tax	.32
		Pay this amount	$5.65

tax for $5.33 as shown on sales tax chart

sum of subtotal and sales tax

Quick Reference

Quantity or **qty.** is the number of items purchased or bought.

Unit price is the cost of one item.

Total cost is Unit Price x Quantity.

The answer in multiplication is called the **product**.

Subtotal is the sum of the amounts in the total-cost column before the sales tax is added.

6% Sales tax means an addition of $.06 on each dollar of purchase. (Many states and cities raise money through sales taxes. The customer pays the tax in the store.) To use the **Sales Tax Chart**, find the subtotal ($5.33) within the two amounts ($5.18–$5.34) shown in the amount-of-sale columns. The sales tax (.32) is at the right of this column.

Alan's Camera Supply

Item Description	Unit Price	Qty.	Total Cost
FILM	5.79	2	
COLOR PRINTS	.36	12	
BATTERIES	2.32	6	
5X7 ENLARGEMENTS	3.15	5	
		Subtotal	
		6% Sales Tax	
		Pay this amount	

Due to space limitations, these answers do not appear in the answer key.

On Your Own

Make a receipt of some things you bought recently. What did you buy? How many? How much did each one cost? How much tax was included in the total amount you paid? Remember: The tax in your state may be different.

Eating Out

When you go out to dinner, first plan ahead. Estimate how much money you think you'll need. Then, when you order, add up the prices of the items you wish to order to make sure you have enough money. When your bill comes, be sure to check your waitperson's math! Don't forget tax and tip (usually 15% of the cost of your meal).

Menu

Entrée
Hamburger $5.00
Cheeseburger. 5.85
Chopped Steak. 7.25
Fried Shrimp 7.50
Broiled Filet of Sole 7.75
Seafood Platter. 8.25

Side Orders
Soup of the Day. 3.75
Side Salad 1.60
Vegetable of the Day 2.55
Cole Slaw 1.35
Onion Rings 1.10
French Fries. 1.00
Baked Potato 1.90

Sandwiches
Egg Salad. 3.50
Tuna 3.95
Turkey 4.25
Chicken Salad 3.75
Ham and Cheese 3.95
Roast Beef 4.50

Desserts
Chocolate Cake 3.65
Apple Pie. 3.79
Cheesecake 3.85
Ice Cream Scoop 1.75
Donut 55

Beverages
Fruit Juice 1.55
Milk 1.00
Hot Chocolate. 1.65
Coffee or Tea 75

Quick Reference

When adding money, remember these steps:
- Line up the decimal points for each amount you are adding.
- Add each column of numbers from right to left.
- The **sum**, or **total**, is the answer to an addition problem.
- To check your answer, add the amounts again, starting with a different number first.

Use what you've learned.

Look at the menu on page 27 to find the price of each item. Write the prices and then add to find the total cost of each meal. The first problem is done for you.

1. Hamburger $5
   Hot Chocolate $1.65
   Total $6.65

2. Tuna Sandwich .... _____
   Soup .... _____
   Apple Pie .... _____
   Total .... _____

3. Ham and Cheese Sandwich ... _____
   Milk .... _____
   Total .... _____

4. Cheeseburger .... _____
   Fruit Juice .... _____
   Total .... _____

5. Roast Beef Sandwich .. _____
   French Fries .... _____
   Hot Chocolate .... _____
   Total .... _____

6. Fried Shrimp .... _____
   Onion Rings .... _____
   Total .... _____

7. Chicken Salad Sandwich ... _____
   Soup .... _____
   Apple Pie .... _____
   Total .... _____

8. Turkey Sandwich ...... _____
   Cole Slaw .... _____
   Fruit Juice .... _____
   Total .... _____

9. Seafood Platter ...... _____
   Vegetable .... _____
   Cheesecake .... _____
   Coffee .... _____
   Total .... _____

10. Chopped Steak .... _____
    Baked Potato .... _____
    Chocolate Cake ...... _____
    Total .... _____

11. Filet of Sole .... _____
    French Fries .... _____
    Side Salad .... _____
    Fruit Juice .... _____
    Total .... _____

On Your Own

List the items that you would like to order. Then compute the total cost of your meal.

_____ _____

_____ _____

_____ _____

_____ _____

Total _____

28

4. How to Save on Transportation

One-way fare? Monthly ticket? Weekly rate? Which is the best buy? This lesson will show you that the number of trips you take affects which fare plan is best for you.

The people in the following exercises are commuters or regular riders on the Intercity Rail. Figure out how much they pay on one-way trips for each fare plan shown on the chart. The first problem is done for you.

INTER*CITY* RAIL

	LOCATION	MONTHLY	WEEKLY	REGULAR ONE-WAY
BARRINGTON TO:	Smithfield	112.00	35.00	5.00
	Lexington	132.00	41.00	6.00
	Madison	143.00	44.00	6.75
	Bakersville	160.00	50.00	7.75
	Los Alamos	175.00	54.00	10.50
	Greenvale	175.00	54.00	10.50

MONTHLY: Good for 60 one-way trips for 1 month.
WEEKLY: Good for 14 one-way trips for 1 week. REGULAR ONE-WAY: Good for 1 one-way trip.

1. Dr. Jose Cortez goes to Smithfield and returns home to Barrington 3 times a week for 1 month.

a. What does the regular one-way ticket cost? *$5*

b. How many one-way trips does he make in 1 week? *6*

c. How much is a weekly ticket? *$35*

d. What is the cost of each trip on the weekly fare plan? *$5.83*

e. How many one-way trips does he make in 1 month? *24*

f. How much is a monthly ticket? *$112*

g. What is the cost of each trip on the monthly fare plan? *$4.67*

h. Which fare plan is cheaper for Dr. Cortez? *MONTHLY*

2. Pat goes to Barrington and back home to Bakersville 5 times a week for 1 month.

a. What does the regular one-way ticket cost? _____

b. How many one-way trips does Pat make in 1 week? _____

c. How much does a weekly ticket cost? _____

d. What is the cost of each trip on the weekly fare plan? _____

e. How many one-way trips are made in 1 month? _____

f. How much is a monthly ticket? _____

g. What is the cost of each trip on the monthly fare plan? _____

h. Which fare plan is cheapest? _____

3. Tyrone makes 14 one-way trips per week between Barrington and Los Alamos.

a. How much is the regular one-way ticket? _____

b. What is the cost of each trip on a weekly ticket? _____

c. How much will Tyrone save if he buys the weekly ticket? (Subtract answer b from answer a.) _____

On Your Own

Pick a place where you might go to work regularly. Ask your local bus company or railroad about special fare plans. Decide which plan is best for you.

Regular one-way fare _____

Monthly rate _____

Number of trips you might make in 1 month _____

Cost of each one-way trip on the monthly fare plan _____

Weekly rate _____

Number of trips you might make in 1 week _____

Cost of each one-way trip on the weekly fare plan _____

5. At the Grocery

"I don't want to buy the whole thing!" What if you only want to buy a half a pound of pork chops? Often the price that is advertised is not for the amount you want to buy. That's when you have to use fractions.

Fresh Grade A Meat

Roast Beef	$6.29 / lb.
Pork Chops	$4.20 / lb.
Chicken	$3.29 / lb.
Turkey	$4.99 / lb.

Cooked Shrimp	7.65 l lb.
Fried Clams	2.99 l lb.
Fresh Salmon	6.49 l lb.

Navel Oranges

Juicy Sweet	12 for $3.10
Watermelon	$3.50 ea.
Pineapple	$4.00 ea.
Cantaloupe	$2.79 ea.

GOLDEN CORN
4 10-OZ. CANS $1.00

Quick Reference
A fraction is a part of a whole.
To find a fractional cost: Multiply the cost of the whole item by the numerator of the fraction. Then divide the result by the denominator.
Example:

$$\frac{1}{2} \times \$1.50 = \frac{1.50}{2} \qquad \frac{1.50}{2} = 2\overline{)1.50} = \$.75$$

$$\begin{array}{r} .75 \\ 2\overline{)1.50} \\ \underline{1.4} \\ 10 \\ \underline{10} \\ 00 \end{array}$$

1	whole	$\frac{3}{4}$	three fourths or three quarters
$\frac{1}{2}$	one half	$\frac{1}{4}$	one fourth or one quarter

---

Use the prices above to compute the total cost of each shopping list below. You may need to figure the fractional cost of an item. We did the first one for you.

1. $\frac{1}{2}$ watermelon   *$1.75*
    1 can of corn   *$.25*
    1 lb. turkey   *$4.99*
           Total   *$6.99*

2. 1 pineapple   _____
    1 lb. chicken   _____
    $\frac{1}{3}$ lb. fried clams   _____
         Total   _____

3. 1 lb. roast beef   _____
    $\frac{3}{4}$ watermelon   _____
    $\frac{1}{2}$ lb. shrimp   _____
         Total   _____

4. 2 cans corn   _____
    6 oranges   _____
    1 lb. chicken   _____
    $\frac{1}{4}$ lb. pork chops   _____
         Total

5. 12 oranges   _____
    1 lb. fried clams   _____
    $\frac{3}{4}$ lb. roast beef   _____
    $\frac{2}{3}$ watermelon   _____
         Total   _____

On Your Own

Go to your grocery store and make a list of the things you want to buy. Then compute the total cost of your shopping list.

E-mail may be faster, but everyone still likes to get real mail. How much does it cost to send a letter or package to friends or family? That depends on what it weighs and where it's going. This lesson will give you practice in reading scales and figuring the cost of priority, first-class, and express mailings.

In the First-Class Mail chart, write the weight shown on the scale for each letter, a–f. Then compute the mailing cost of a first-class rate of $.34 for the first ounce (oz.) or fraction of an ounce, and $.23 for each additional ounce or fraction up to 11 ounces. Letter d is done for you.

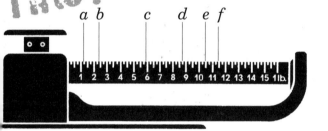

a b   c   d e f

First-Class Mail

Written letters and other sealed matter may be sent by first-class mail.

Letter	Weight	Cost of 1st Oz. or Fraction	Cost of Additional Oz. or Fraction	Total Cost
a				
b				
c				
d	$8\frac{1}{2}$ oz.	$.34	$8\frac{1}{2}$ oz. – 1ST oz. = $7\frac{1}{2}$ oz. 8 X .23 = $1.84	$.34 + $1.84 = $2.18
e				
f				

On Your Own

Packages weighing 16 ounces or more, but not more than 40 pounds, may be mailed by parcel post or fourth-class mail. Rates are based on weight, but they also vary according to distance. Next time you mail packages to friends or relatives, ask for the rates at the parcel-post window in your post office. Use the following chart to record the cost of the packages you send.

To Whom	Where	Weight	Cost

Priority Mail

Items that are too heavy to send by first-class mail may be sent by priority mail. The cost depends on what zone the item, up to 70 pounds, is being mailed to.

Use the table below to determine the mailing cost of g–l at priority-class rate to the zone indicated.

Weight up to but not over	Local 1, 2, & 3	4	5	6	7	8
2 lb.	3.50					
3 lb.	3.95					
4 lb.	6.35					
5 lb.	6.50					
10 lb.	7.00	8.50	9.50	11.25	12.50	15.25
15 lb.	8.50	11.70	13.30	15.85	17.50	21.70
20 lb.	10.35	14.85	17.00	20.40	22.65	28.20
70 lb.	28.70	46.55	53.95	66.00	73.00	88.80

Mail	Weight	Zone	Total Cost
g	15 oz.	7	
h	3 lb.	3	
i	70 lb.	8	
j	4 lb. 2 oz.	1	
k	20 lb.	5	
l	1 lb. 4 oz.	4	

Putting It All Together

1. Write a check for one dinner that includes the following: shrimp cocktail—$4.35, steak—$8.66, apple pie—$3.75, and tea—$1.10. Add 5% sales tax. Compute the total bill.

2. Your cash balance on Monday morning was $100. Your daily expenses from Monday to Friday were: $28.50, $6.88, $32.69, $17.34, and $10.25, respectively. How much money did you have at the end of each day? What was your end-of-week balance?

3. Fill out a sales receipt for 3 pens—$.39 each, 1 legal pad—$1.50 each, 2 notebooks—$2.75 each, and 4 pencils—$.25 each. Include 8% sales tax. Compute the total receipt.

4. How much will a $.69 item cost with sales tax in the following four cities?
   Toronto   8%
   New York City   8.25%
   San Francisco   6.25%
   Houston   7.25%

5. A monthly ticket, which is good for 60 trips, costs $143. A weekly ticket, valid for 14 trips, costs $44. The regular one-way fare is $6.75. Which ticket should the following people buy?

   a. Suzie Tan who makes 42 trips a month.

   b. Felix Santos who goes to work and returns home 3 times a week.

6. A sack of rice costs $14.70. Write the cost of $\frac{3}{4}, \frac{2}{3}, \frac{1}{2}, \frac{1}{3},$ and $\frac{1}{4}$ of the sack.

7. What is the difference in cost between the following two calls?

   a. To Boston, Massachusetts, on Tuesday at 12 noon for 10 minutes. The initial 3-minute charge is $2.85 and each additional minute costs $.29.

   Init. 3 min.   _____
   Add. 7 min.   _____
   Total cost   _____

   b. To Boston, Massachusetts, on Sunday at 12 noon for 10 minutes. The initial 1-minute charge is $.40 and each additional minute costs $.12.

   Init. 1 min.   _____
   Add. 9 min.   _____
   Total cost   _____

   The difference in cost is   _____

8. In the chart below, write the weight shown on the scale for each letter. Compute the mailing cost for a first-class rate of $.34 for the first ounce or fraction and $.23 for each additional ounce or fraction. Each mark represents a quarter of an ounce. Due to space limitations, these answers do not appear in the answer key.

Letter	Weight	Cost
a		
b		
c		
d		
e		

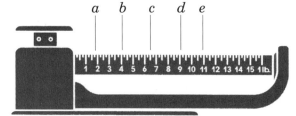

You have seen how useful math skills are in your daily activities. The exercises in this section will help sharpen your skills.

Add.

1.   10
       5
    + 204

2.   457
     3214
       62
     +135

3. $29.75
    6.82
    .49
   +2.63

4. $10.00
   131.16
    .08
   +40.05

5. $4.55 + $.89 + $24.50 = _____

Subtract.

6. 6879
   −2765

7.   341
    −265

8. $8.25
   −4.15

9. $25.43
   −9.39

10. $128.78 − $32.69 = _____

Multiply.

11. 2743
    x 50

12. 2135
    x 32

13. .87
    x3

14. 65.23
    x.05

15. 4.35 x .25 = _____

Divide.

16. 2)848

17. 32)3968

18. 26)55.90

19. 13)19.50

20. 164.30 ÷ 62 = _____

Round each answer to the nearest penny.

21. $5.14
    x .03

22. $7.32
    x .06

23. 5)$61.32

24. 32)$73.40

25. $101.60 ÷ 48 = _____

26. 8% of $125 =
27. 20% of $184.56 =
28. 9% of $105.32 =

29. $\frac{2}{3}$ of $9.72 =
30. $\frac{3}{4}$ of $8.35 =
31. $\frac{1}{2}$ of $253.64 =
32. $\frac{1}{4}$ of $672.87 =

On Your Own

A. Find out how a taxi meter works. Ask a local taxi driver how much the first fraction of a mile costs and how much each additional fraction is. Figure the total cost of distances you might want to travel.

B. Taxi drivers, waiters, bell hops, and others who offer some kind of service usually receive a tip. Find out how much tip is given in your community. Practice making quick estimates so that you can give the correct tip the next time someone serves you.

Your Money and Math

section **3**

When **budgeting** for your **expenses**, be sure to take care of necessities first. That way it's easier to save up for the things you've always dreamed about owning.

Contents

1. Checking Account 35

2. Balancing Your Checkbook 37

3. Savings 39

4. Budgeting 41

5. Renting an Apartment 43

6. Are You Covered? 45

7. All About Credit 46

8. Filing Your Income Tax 48

9. Putting It All Together 50

   Skills Survey 52

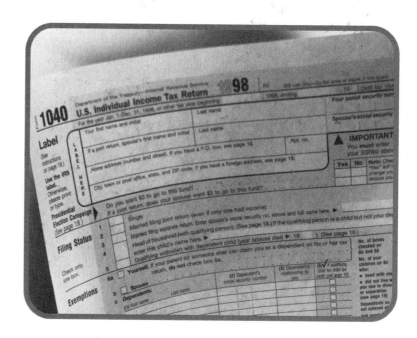

1. Checking Account

In this lesson, you will learn the basic steps of **managing your money** in a checking account. Math makes it simple.

Quick Reference

With a checking account, you can deposit money and then take it out by writing a check. To fill out a deposit slip, follow these steps:

1. Write the date
2. Write your name
3. Count the cash you are depositing and write the amount on the **CASH** line.
4. On the **CHECK** lines, list the amount of each check you are depositing.
5. Add the cash and the check lines to find the **TOTAL** deposit.

To write a check, follow these steps:

1. Fill in the date.

2. Write the name of the person or company to be paid.

3. Write the amount of the check in numerals with the cents shown as a fraction of 100 (example: 58/100).

4. Write the dollar amount in words (example: fourteen) and the cents again as a fraction of 100.

5. Write what you are paying for on the "memo" line.

6. Sign the check.

	No. 291		Stella Uribe		No. 291
	April 7 20*02*			*April 7* 20 02	
To *M. Scott and Son*					
For			Pay to the order of *M. Scott and Son*	$ 5.63	
			five and ———————— 63/100	Dollars	
Bal Fwd:	$189.60		**Nickel Bank and Trust Co.**		
Amt Deposited:	10.00		Main Street		
Total:	199.60				
Amt This Check:	5.63		memo *paint bill*	*Stella Uribe*	
Bal:	$193.97		:027::091:447259:291		

Fill out the deposit slips for the deposits described in 1–2.

1. You have a 10 dollar bill, a 20 dollar bill, and 52 cents. You also want to deposit checks for $40.50 and $14.15.

DEPOSIT SLIP
Nickel Bank and Trust Co.

Name _____

Date _____

Checking
Account # _____

		Dollars	Cents
Cash			
Checks	1		
	2		
	3		
Bank use only	Total		

2. Your cash deposit includes $10, $5, $20 and $.75. The checks are $5.98, $15, and $76.83.

DEPOSIT SLIP

Date _____

Checking Account # _____

Name _____

		Dollars	Cents
Cash			
Checks	1		
	2		
	3		
	4		
Bank Use only	5		
	Total		

Write the checks for the payments described in 3–5.

3. On Sept. 5, 2001, you bought a portable CD player from Grand Sound, Inc., for $89.95.

No. 292

_____ 20____

Pay to the order of _____ $ _____

_____ Dollars

United Money Bank
Main Street

memo _____

:027::091:447259:292

4. On Oct. 7, 2001, you bought a watch from Fine Jewel Co., for $183.97.

No. 293

_____ 20____

Pay to the order of _____ $ _____

_____ Dollars

United Money Bank
Main Street

memo _____

:027::091:447259:293

5. You cashed a check for $25 on Nov. 10, 2001. (Write "Cash" on the line marked "Pay to the order of.")

No. 294

_____ 20____

Pay to the order of _____ $ _____

_____ Dollars

United Money Bank
Main Street

memo _____

:027::091:447259:294

On Your Own

Fill out a deposit slip for the cash and checks you may want to put into your checking account. Write a check for a bill you might pay.

2. Balancing Your Checkbook

What piece of paper can "bounce"? You guessed it—a check! If you write a check for an amount that is more than the total amount that you have in your account, your check will bounce. That means the check is not good and will be returned to you by your bank. You will still have to pay the amount you owe, plus an additional amount to the bank as a penalty charge. This lesson will help you avoid the bounce dilemma by keeping track of the money in your account using a check register.

Quick Reference
This is a page from a **check register**.

CHECK NO.	DATE	CHECK ISSUED TO OR DESCRIPTION OF DEPOSIT	DEPOSITS AMOUNT	AMOUNT OF CHECK	✓ T	BALANCE	

Each time you write a check or make an ATM (automatic teller machine) withdrawal, fill out the check register following these steps:

1. Write the check number or "ATM withdrawal."

2. Write the date.

3. Write the name of the person or company you paid, or "cash" if you used an ATM.

4. Write what the check or withdrawal was for.

5. Write the amount of the check or withdrawal.

6. Subtract the amount of the check or withdrawal from the old balance and enter the new balance in your register.

ATM fees are often charged when you withdraw money using your ATM card at a bank other than your own. Be sure to keep track of ATM fees in your check register.

Each time you make a deposit, follow these steps:

1. Write the date of the deposit.

2. Write "deposit" and a description of the deposit (for example, "paycheck" or "gift").

3. Write the total amount you deposited.

4. Add the deposit to the old balance and enter the new balance in your register.

Fill out the following check register for the payments and deposits listed below it.
Due to space limitations, these answers do not appear in the answer key.

CHECK NO.	DATE	CHECK ISSUED TO OR DESCRIPTION OF DEPOSIT	DEPOSITS AMOUNT	AMOUNT OF CHECK	✓T	BALANCE

151	Feb. 1	Sands Realty Co. (Rent) . .	$250.00	
152	Feb. 5	National Telephone	15.25	
153	Feb. 10	Franklin Electric	13.43	
154	Feb. 14	The Flower Shop (Gift)	8.50	
	Feb. 15	Deposit (Paycheck)	198.52	
ATM	Feb. 17	Cash (Lunch money)	25.00	
ATM	Feb. 17	Fee for cash withdrawal	1.00	
155	Feb. 19	Dr. T. Lightfoot (Dentist)	20.00	
156	Feb. 20	Alex Fashions (Clothes)	38.50	
157	Feb. 21	Pantry Kitchen (Groceries) . .	52.18	
158	Feb. 22	United Oil Co. (Gas credit card)	27.58	
ATM	Feb. 25	Cash (Movies)	25.00	
ATM	Feb. 25	Fee for cash withdrawal	1.00	
	Feb. 28	Deposit (Paycheck)	198.52	

On Your Own

Record the deposits and checks you think you might make the first month you are "on your own."

CHECK NO.	DATE	CHECK ISSUED TO OR DESCRIPTION OF DEPOSIT	DEPOSITS AMOUNT	AMOUNT OF CHECK	✓T	BALANCE

Saving for a holiday? New clothes, perhaps? Regular deposits of money in a **bank savings account** is one way to save. It's safe and your money earns **interest**. In this lesson you will learn to use a savings account and to find the simple interest your money can earn.

Quick Reference

You will receive a **monthly statement** from your bank, listing your deposits, withdrawals, and interest earned.

Deposits are added to the balance.

Withdrawals are subtracted from the balance.

Interest is usually credited or added quarterly on March 31, June 30, September 30, and December 31.

Interest = Balance x rate x time. The interest rate for the account below is 5% yearly. The interest for March 31 is computed like this:

$$\text{Interest} = (100 \times .05) \times \tfrac{1}{4} \text{ year}$$
$$= 5.00 \times \tfrac{1}{4}$$
$$= \frac{5.00}{4}$$
$$\text{Interest} = \$1.25$$

Use the information on the monthly account statement below to answer the following questions. The first on is done for you.

1. On January 1, Eleanor deposited $100 in her bank account. After earning interest for the first quarter, she had $101.25. What is the rate of interest on the account?

   $101.25 – $100 =   *$1.25*

   $1.25 ÷ $100 =   *.0125*

   .0125 x 4 quarters =   *.05 OR 5%*

2. If Eleanor leaves her $91.25 in the account for the rest of the year (9 months), how much interest will she earn?

   _____

3. How much total interest will she earn for the year?

   _____

| In Account with:
ELEANOR S. ANGELES | | | | Account Number
10-49104-1 | |
DATE	WITHDRAWAL	DEPOSIT	INTEREST OR DIVIDEND	BALANCE	TELLER
1-1-02		100.00		100.00	16B
3-31-02			1.25	101.25	14A
4-1-02	10.00			91.25	

Read the facts carefully and then answer questions 1–3.

1. a. Suppose you open an account on January 1 with a deposit of $64. How much interest will your money earn at the end of the quarter (March 31) at an interest rate of 5% yearly?

    _____

    b. What is your new balance on April 1?

    _____

    c. If you don't make any deposits or withdrawals, how much interest will this new balance earn at the end of the next quarter (June 30)?

    _____

Due to space limitations, the answers to questions 2 and 3 do not appear in the answer key.

2. You want to withdraw $30.50 from your account on July 1. Fill out this withdrawal slip. Use 10-49104-1 as your account number.

WITHDRAWAL	THE PASSBOOK MUST BE PRESENTED WITH THIS ORDER.
	_____ 20 ____ ACCOUNT NUMBER _____
	PAY TO MYSELF OR BEARER
	_____ DOLLARS
	PLEASE WRITE AMOUNT
	signature_____
	INDIVIDUALLY OR IN A REPRESENTATIVE CAPACITY AS THE BOOK READS.

3. The interest (5% yearly) and balance amounts are missing from this statement. Fill them in.

DEPOSITORS NAME ON PAGE ONE			Account Number 10-49104-1	
DATE	WITHDRAWAL	DEPOSIT	INTEREST OR DIVIDEND	BALANCE
Jan 1		400.00		....
Mar 30			....	....
Apr 1	65.00			....
Jun 30			....	....
Jul 1		75.75		....
Sep 30			....	....

Fill in this statement with the deposits and withdrawals you might make during a three-month period.

DEPOSITORS NAME ON PAGE ONE			Account Number 10-49104-1	
DATE	WITHDRAWAL	DEPOSIT	INTEREST OR DIVIDEND	BALANCE
Jan 1		400.00		....
Mar 30			....	....
Apr 1	65.00			....
Jun 30			....	....
Jul 1		75.75		....
Sep 30			....	....

Earning money may be hard, but spending it is very easy! That's why it's important to have a **budget**. When you create your own budget, be sure to take care of what you really need first. Then it's easier to save up for the things you've always wanted. This lesson is all about setting up a budget, managing your money, and mastering the math you need to do it.

Before creating your own budget, get some practice managing someone else's money. Fill out the budget sheet in questions 1 and 2. First, find the total amount needed for fixed expenses. Then adjust the flexible expenses so that each person can save money.

Write down how much each one could save, and give suggestions of where they can trim their spending.

1. Linda earns $375 a week as a proofreader. Her net income per week is $236.50. Here is a list of her expenses last month.

Lunches	$60.00
Movies	16.00
Rent	395.00
Haircut	17.00
Telephone	32.42
Electricity	13.50
Clothes	61.00
Transportation	30.00
Groceries	72.50
Loan Payment	53.08
Cleaners	10.50

Linda wants to save. Help her decide which expenses to cut down.

Net Monthly Income. . . . **236.50 X 4 = $946.00**

Fixed Expenses

RENT	$395.00
LOAN PAYMENT	53.08
TRANSPORTATION	30.00
TELEPHONE	32.42
ELECTRICITY	13.50

Total Fixed Expenses	$524.00
Balance	$422

Quick Reference

BUDGETING TIPS:

- Find out how much you actually take home each month: Net monthly income = 4 x amount of weekly paycheck or 2 x amount of biweekly paycheck.

- Deduct from your net monthly income all fixed expenses (those that are the same or nearly the same each month), such as rent, utilities (gas and electric), telephone, fuel bill, transportation, etc.

- Adjust your flexible expenses (those which may vary more or are not needed each month) based on the money you have available after deducting the fixed expenses. Decide what you need to spend for such things as food, health care, clothing, entertainment, etc.

- Don't forget to include some money for savings and emergencies.

Now Linda can use some of the balance for Flexible Expenses.

Flexible Expenses

CLOTHES	$61.00
MOVIES	$16.00

Total Flexible Expenses	$77.00

Savings $ _____

Suggested Spending Adjustments $_____

2. Tim's job at the record store pays $200 a week. His actual take-home pay is $165. Here is a list of Tim's expenses last month.

Entertainment $80.00
Rent 255.00
Telephone 29.50
Gifts 20.00
Food 60.00
Car Payment 68.13
Gas & Repairs 40.00
Clothing. 50.00
Electricity. 12.37
Dentist. 25.00

Tim wants to go to night school. He needs to save at least $100 a month. Help him work out a budget.

Net Monthly Income . . . . $ _____

Fixed Expenses . . . . $ _____

. . . . _____

. . . . _____

. . . . _____

. . . . _____

Total Fixed Expenses $ _____

Balance $ _____

Flexible Expenses

. . . . _____

. . . . _____

. . . . _____

. . . . _____

Total Flexible Expenses $ _____

Savings. . . . . $ _____

Suggested Spending . . . . $ _____

Adjustments . . . . $ _____

On Your Own

Now it's time to budget your own money. How much do you receive each month? Remember, take care of what you *really* need first. Then, assign what's left to your other expenses. If you want to save for something special, you can do it! Just work out your budget and stick to it.

Net Monthly Income . . . . $ _____

Fixed Expenses. . . . . $ _____

. . . . _____

. . . . _____

. . . . _____

. . . . _____

Total Fixed Expenses $ _____

Balance $ _____

Flexible Expenses

. . . . _____

. . . . _____

. . . . _____

Total Flexible Expenses $ _____

Savings. . . . . $ _____

Suggested Spending. . . . . $ _____

Adjustments . . . . $ _____

Quick Reference

The following abbreviations and words are often used in ads.

A/C: Air conditioned

Apt: Apartment

Bdrm or BR: Bedroom

Bldg: Building

Brkr: Broker (company or person who gets a fee for finding an apartment—which usually means you pay them an amount equal to one or two month's rent)

Bth: Bathroom

D/W: Dishwasher

Effcy: Efficiency (one room with kitchen and bath)

Flr: Floor

Furn: Furnished or with furniture

Immed occup: Immediate occupancy (you can move in now)

Incl: Including

Kit: Kitchen

Livrm or LR: Living room

Lge: Large

Lse: Lease (a legal contract to stay in apartment for a given period)

Mod: Modern

Nr: Near

Rm: Room

Sec: Security (usually equal to one-month's rent to cover any damages you might cause in the apartment. You get it back at the end of your lease.)

Sml: Small

Studio: Similar to an efficiency apartment

Sublet: To rent an apartment from someone who's already renting it

Supt: Superintendent

Util: Utilities (gas, heat, electricity)

W/D: Washer & Dryer in apartment unit

Looking for an apartment can be like decoding a secret message. All the codes in the ads are about **rent**, **fees**, and other **expenses**. If you take some time to learn exactly what the ads say, finding the actual cost of renting a home is no great mystery!

Which apartment should the people in questions 1–2 rent? Read the facts about each and then help them choose. Remember to include transportation costs in making your decision. The first problem is done for you.

1. Rose Chan's net monthly income is $1,800. She wants to rent either apartment A or B. She can walk to work from A, but the utilities will cost her at least $45 a month. She has to ride from B at $1 a ride for 40 trips a month.

CLASSIFIED

APARTMENTS FOR RENT

A **Main St. Studio.** Lge rm with kit & bth. $590 plus util. Call eves. 672-4785.

B **UPTOWN EFFCY.** Luxury apt with livrm, kit, and full bth. $590 incl util. Call Supt. 699-9424.

Actual Costs	A	B
Rent	$590	$590
Utilities	45	0
Transportation	0	40
TOTAL MONTHLY COSTS	$635	$630

Can Rose pay the total cost for each apartment? YES

Which apartment should she rent based on cost? B

43

2. Jimmy Santos's weekly paycheck is $314 or _____ monthly. His budget for rent and transportation is 35% of his monthly income. How much is this? _____ Utilities cost about $25 a month. Jimmy can walk to work from apartment B. The cost of transportation from apartment A is $1.50 a trip, and Jimmy makes at least 40 trips a month.

Actual Costs	A	B
Rent	_____	_____
Utilities	_____	_____
Transportation	_____	_____
TOTAL MONTHLY COST	_____	_____

Can Jimmy pay the total monthly cost for each apartment? _____

Which apartment should Jimmy rent based on cost? _____

A **Broad & 16th (southside)** 1 BR, Lr, bth, eat-in kit incl util. $400/month 332-0687

B **Snyder & Hunting Park (north)** 1st flr, mod, 3 rms. $400/month plus util. 485-2327.

On Your Own

You have a choice between the two apartments at right. Apartment A is within a one-ride zone, so that a one-way trip to work will cost only $1. Apartment B requires two rides of $1 each time you go to work. The average cost of utilities for each is $19.

A 1 BR Apt North Hills. Mod, furn, nr park. High flr. Immed occup. $450 plus util.

B 1 Bdrm Apt South Shore Lge rms, kit with d/w. $390 plus util. Avail Jan 1

Actual Costs	A	B
Rent	_____	_____
Utilities	_____	_____
Transportation	_____	_____
TOTAL MONTHLY COST	_____	_____

Which apartment should you rent based on cost? _____

Quick Reference

Insurance: A way of protecting yourself and your family against an emergency. For instance, if you get sick, the insurance company will pay for all or part of your medical bills.

Policy: The agreement between you and the insurance company. It usually shows what your insurance covers.

Premium: The amount you pay for the benefits promised to you.

Deductible: A fixed amount of medical costs you pay. Any amount over the deductible amount will be paid by the insurance company.

Being sick can be very expensive. A serious accident or illness could use up a lifetime of savings! That's why people buy **medical insurance.** In this lesson you will discover the cost and benefits of being covered by medical insurance.

In questions 1–2, compute the amount you would have to pay for each medical case using the information provided about each insurance plan in the table. We started the activity for you.

	Plan A	Plan B	Plan C	Plan D
Monthly Premiums	$39	48	63	75
Maximum Benefits Per Illness:				
Hospital room and board (per day)	$60	75	105	150
Doctor's bills (deductible)	$400	200	150	none
X-ray and lab fees	$30	75	150	full
Anesthesiologist	$45	75	120	full
Drugs	$30	60	105	150
Nursing services	25%	33%	50%	75%

1. CAR CRASH

	Actual Cost	Plan C Insurance Pays	You Pay
Hospital room and board (4 days at $180)	$720 (4 x 105)	420 (720–420)	$300
Doctor's bill	400 (–150 deductible)	250 (400–250)	150
Anesthesiologist	250	120 (25–120)	130
X-rays	200	150	50
Drugs	50	50	0
Nursing services	250 (50% of 250)	125 (250–125)	125
TOTAL	$1870	$1195	$755

2. GENERAL PHYSICAL EXAMINATION & MEDICAL TESTS

	Actual Cost	Plan D Insurance Pays	You Pay
Hospital room and board (2 days at $100)	$200	120	$80
Doctor's bill	150	150	
X-rays	75	30	45
TOTAL	$425	$150	$275

On Your Own

Insurance and medical costs can be much more expensive than the prices you see here, depending on things like your age, health, and the state in which you live. Talk to an insurance agent about a medical plan for you. How large a monthly premium can you include in your budget? List the benefits you can expect from your policy.

Due to space limitations, these answers do not appear in the answer key.

7. All About Credit

You just discovered that you do not have enough money to buy something you really need. Should you borrow from a friend? Or should you borrow from a bank? In either case, you are using credit. This lesson is all about credit and how to use it wisely.

When you use credit, you have to pay extra for it. If you buy the items in questions 1–3 on credit, how much more will you pay? The first question is done for you.

1. MINI-REFRIGERATOR
$350 cash or $50 down and
$28/month for 12 months

Total amount of payments	$386
Less cash price	$350
Cost of credit	$36

2. DVD PLAYER
$27.50 monthly for 1 year or
$270.95 cash

Total amount of payments	_____
Less cash price	_____
Cost of credit	_____

3. DESKTOP COMPUTER
12 monthly payments of $120
or $1100 cash

Total amount of payments	_____
Less cash price	_____
Cost of credit	_____

Loans

Which loan is cheaper? Find the rate of interest paid for 1 month on each loan in question. Use the method shown in this example.

Example: What is the interest rate on a $300 loan for 5 months with an interest charge of $30?

$$\text{Rate} = \frac{\text{Interest}}{\text{Amount of loan} \times \text{time}}$$
$$= \frac{\$30}{\$300 \times 5}$$
$$= \frac{\$30}{\$1500}$$

Rate = .02 or 2% a month

4. Which of these loans has the lowest rate of interest?
  a. $500 with an interest charge of $50 fully paid after 10 months.
       Rate = _____
  b. $400 with an interest charge of $40 fully paid after 5 months.
       Rate = _____
  c. $600 with an interest charge of $43.20 fully paid after 6 months.
       Rate = _____

Quick Reference

Finance charge or **interest**: The amount of money to be paid in addition to the principal or amount borrowed.

Down payment: The cash to be paid at the time something is purchased on credit.

Credit card: A plastic card that can be used like money.

To get a credit card, you must sign a contract called a **Retail Installment Credit Agreement**. Read it carefully before you sign!

Use the Retail Installment Credit Agreement below when answering questions 5–7.

RETAIL INSTALLMENT CREDIT AGREEMENT

I may, within 25 days of the closing date appearing on the periodic statement of my account, pay in full the "new balance" appearing on said statement and thereby avoid a FINANCE CHARGE; or, if I so choose, I may pay my account in monthly installments in accordance with the schedule below. If I avail myself of the latter option, I will incur and pay a FINANCE CHARGE computed at a periodic rate of $1\frac{1}{2}$ % per month (an ANNUAL PERCENTAGE RATE of 18%) on that portion of the previous balance which does not exceed $500.00 (subject to a minimum charge of 50¢) and 1% per month (an ANNUAL PERCENTAGE CHARGE on balances of $5.00 or less. The FINANCE CHARGE will be computed on the previous balance without deducting any payments or other credits and without adding current purchases.

Notice to the buyer: 1. Do not sign this credit agreement before you read it or if it contains any blank space. 2. You are entitled to a completely filled in copy of this credit agreement at the time you sign it. 3. You may at any time pay your total indebtedness hereunder. 4. Keep this agreement to protect your legal rights.

PAYMENT	If indebtedness is	$.01 to 10.00	$10.01 to 60.00	$60.01 to 90.00	$90.01 to 120.00	$120.01 to 180.00	$180.01 to 240.00	Over $240.00
	Monthly Payment is	Full Balance	$10.00	$15.00	$20.00	$30.00	$40.00	1/5 of Balance

APPROVED BY: _____   BUYER'S SIGNATURE _____

5. What is the finance charge on a debt of $80 for 1 month?
(Remember: Interest = amount borrowed x rate in decimal form x time.)

_____

6. You bought $46 worth of books and CDs. You want to pay the full amount next month, including interest. How much do you have to pay?

_____

7. a. Your last credit card bill shows that you owe a total of $150. You paid the minimum of $30. How much more do you owe?

_____

b. What will be the interest added next month?

_____

![dotted line decoration]

On Your Own

If you don't have a credit card yet, you will probably apply for one soon. If you do, remember to be careful and spend wisely. Some credit cards offer very low interest rates for the first few months, and then increase the interest rate dramatically.

Why do you think credit card companies do this?

8. Filing Your Income Tax

Once you get a job, you must file an **income tax form** every year. It's not as difficult as many tax experts want you to believe! This lesson will show you how to fill out an income tax form using the information on your **W-2 form** and **tax tables.**

Follow the instructions below to complete the income tax form on page 49 for a single with no dependents.

A. Print your name and address.

B. Write your social security number. (If you don't have one, use the social security number shown on the W-2 form below.)

C. On the W-2 form, find the dollar amount in the box marked "Wages, tips, and other compensation." Write the amount on line 1.

D. You saved $400 at 6% interest rate this year. Find the interest you earned (amount x rate in decimal form) and write amount in line 2.

E. Add lines 1 and 2. This is your adjusted gross income.

F. Check the box for "no." Write the standard deduction on line 5.

G. Subtract line 5 from line 4 and write the difference on line 6.

H. On the W-2 form, find the amount in the box marked "Federal income tax withheld." Write the amount on line 7.

I. Write the amount on line 7 on line 9 also.

J. Look at the tax table. In the first column, find the line that matches the amount you wrote on line 6. Go over to the column marked single. Write the amount you see on line 10.

K. Subtract the amounts listed on lines 9 and 10. Read lines 11 and 12 and write the difference on the correct line.

L. Be sure to sign and date the bottom section.

W-2 Wage and Tax Statement

1. Control Number	2222			
		OMB no. 1545-0008		
2. Employer's name, address, and ZIP code		3. Employer's identification Number		4. Employer's State I.D. number
Scholastic 1290 Wall Street West Lyndhurst, NJ 07071		5. Statutory employee ☐ Deceased ☐ Pension plan ☐ Legal rep. ☐ 942 emp. ☐ Subtotal ☐ Deferred compensation ☐ Void ☐		
		6. Allocated Tips		7. Advanced EIC payment
8. Employee's social security number 012-34-5678	9. Federal income tax withheld 1,345.00	10. Wages, tips, other compensation 13,500.00		11. Social security tax withheld 1,014.00
12. Employee's name, address, ZIP Code		13. Social security wages 13,500.00		14. Social security tips
Joe Smith 16 W. 22 Street New York, NY 10012		16.		16a. Fringe benefits incl. Box 10
		17. State income tax 675	18. State wages, tips, etc. 13,500.00	19. Name of state
		20. Local income tax	21. Local wages, tips, etc	22. Name of locality

If Form 1040EZ, line 6, is—		And you are—	
At least	But less than	Single	Married filing jointly
		Your tax is—	
8,000			
8,000	8,050	1,204	1,204
8,050	8,100	1,211	1,211
8,100	8,150	1,219	1,219
8,150	8,200	1,226	1,226
8,200	8,250	1,234	1,234
8,250	8,300	1,241	1,241
8,300	8,350	1,249	1,249
8,350	8,400	1,256	1,256
8,400	8,450	1,264	1,264
8,450	8,500	1,271	1,271
8,500	8,550	1,279	1,279
8,550	8,600	1,286	1,286
8,600	8,650	1,294	1,294
8,650	8,700	1,301	1,301
8,700	8,750	1,309	1,309
8,750	8,800	1,316	1,316

Due to space limitations, these answers do not appear in the answer key.

Form 1040EZ-I

Department of the Treasury—Internal Revenue Service

Income Tax Return for Single and Joint Filers With No Dependents

2000 OMB No. 1545-0675

A

Use the IRS label here

Your first name and initial | Last name

If a joint return, spouse's first name and initial | Last name

Home address (number and street). If you have a P.O. box, see page 12. | Apt. no.

City, town or post office, state, and ZIP code. If you have a foreign address, see page 12.

B

Your social security number

Spouse's social security number

Presidential Campaign (p. 12)

Note. Checking "Yes" will not change your tax or reduce your refund.
Do you, or spouse if a joint return, want $3 to go to this fund? ▶

You — ☐ Yes ☐ No   Spouse — ☐ Yes ☐ No

Income

Attach Form(s) W-2 here. Enclose, but do not attach, any payment.

1 Total wages, salaries, and tips. This should be shown in box 1 of your W-2 form(s). Attach your W-2 form(s). — 1

2 Taxable interest. If the total is over $400, you cannot use Form 1040EZ. — 2

3 Unemployment compensation, qualified state tuition program earnings, and Alaska Permanent Fund dividends (see page 14). — 3

4 Add lines 1, 2, and 3. This is your **adjusted gross income.** — 4

Note. You **must** check Yes or No

5 Can your parents (or someone else) claim you on their return?

Yes. Enter amount from worksheet on back. ☐

No. If **single,** enter 7,200.00. If **married,** enter 12,950.00. See back for explanation. ☐ — 5

6 Subtract line 5 from line 4. If line 5 is larger than line 4, enter 0. This is your **taxable income.** ▶ 6

Payments and tax

7 Enter your Federal income tax withheld from box 2 of your W-2 form(s). — 7

8a **Earned income credit (EIC).** See page 15.
b Nontaxable earned income: enter type and amount below.
Type _____ $ _____ — 8a

9 Add lines 7 and 8a. These are your **total payments.** — 9

10 **Tax.** Use the amount on **line 6 above** to find your tax in the tax table on pages 24–28 of the booklet. Then, enter the tax from the table on this line. — 10

Refund

Have it directly deposited! See page 20 and fill in 11b, 11c, and 11d.

11a If line 9 is larger than line 10, subtract line 10 from line 9. This is your **refund.** — 11a

b Routing number

c Type: Checking ☐ Savings ☐

d Account number

Amount you owe

12 If line 10 is larger than line 9, subtract line 9 from line 10. This is the **amount you owe.** See page 21 for details on how to pay. — 12

Dollars | Cents

C D E F G H I J K K

I have read this return. Under penalties of perjury, I declare that to the best of my knowledge and belief, the return is true, correct, and accurately lists all amounts and sources of income I received during the tax year.

Sign here ▶

Keep copy for your records.

Your signature | Spouse's signature if joint return. See page 11.

Date | Your occupation | Date | Spouse's occupation

For Official Use Only

1 2 3 4 5
6 7 8 9 10

L

May the IRS discuss this return with the preparer shown on back (see page 21)? ☐ Yes ☐ No

For Disclosure, Privacy Act, and Paperwork Reduction Act Notice, see page 23. Cat. No. 28807B   **2000 Form 1040EZ-I**

49

Putting It All Together

Due to space limitations, the answers to questions 1, 3, and 9 do not appear in the answer key.

1. Fill out this deposit slip for $25 cash and checks for $48.50 and $28.95.

DEPOSIT SLIP

Date _____

Checking Account # _____

Name _____

		Dollars	Cents
Cash			
Checks	1		
	2		
	3		
	4		
Bank Use only	5		
	Total		

2. Write a check for $15 to the Parking Violations Bureau to pay for a parking ticket.

No. 291

_____ 20 _____

Pay to the order of _____ $ _____

_____ Dollars

United Money Bank
Main Street

memo _____   _____

:027::091:447259:291

3. Enter the deposit and check amounts from questions 1–2 in this check register.

CHECK NO.	DATE	CHECK ISSUED TO OR DESCRIPTION OF DEPOSIT	DEPOSITS AMOUNT	AMOUNT OF CHECK	✓ T	BALANCE

4. You opened a savings account with a deposit of $200. If you keep the money in the account for 90 days, how much interest will it earn at a rate of 6% annually?

_____

5. You earn $275 a week and your take-home pay is $225. About how much do you take home each month?

_____

Fill out the budget sheet below as if your usual expenses are the following:

Rent	$275
Clothing	50
Groceries	60
Loan payment	45
Grooming	27
Utilities	25
Telephone	12
Movies and lunches	60
Net Monthly Income	$_____

Fixed Expenses:

_____ _____

_____ _____

_____ _____

_____ _____

Flexible Expenses: _____ _____

_____ _____

_____ _____

_____ _____

TOTAL FIXED EXPENSES	_____ $
TOTAL FLEXIBLE EXPENSES	$_____
BALANCE	$_____
Savings	$_____
Suggested Spending Adjustments	_____

6. Your net monthly income is $1,100 a month. Your combined rent and transportation budget is $400. Utilities in your town usually cost $25 a month. Choose between the two apartments at right. You can walk to work from A. To ride to work from B costs $1, and you need to make at least 50 trips a month.

   Which apartment should you rent? _____

A	44th & 7th Studio. Walk to work from this lge rm with kit & bth. $375 plus util.
B	84th & 10th Effcy Lvrm, sleeping area, full kit & bth. $375 incl. util.

---

7. You have a hospitalization plan that pays a maximum benefit of $208 a day for room and board. You are hospitalized for 5 days at $260 a day. How much is the total hospital bill?_____

   How much will the insurance company pay?

   _____

   How much do you pay? _____

8. You can pay for an electronic organizer with $39.95 in cash. Instead, you decide to pay $4.60 a month for 10 months. How much more do you have to pay?

   _____

---

9. Look at the amounts on lines 9 and 10 on this part of an income tax form. On which line should you write the difference between these two amounts? Line 11 or 12? _____

   Write the amount on the correct line.

Payments and tax	7 Enter your Federal income tax withheld from box 2 of your W-2 form(s). 7	9 084 00
	8a **Earned income credit (EIC).** See page 15. b Nontaxable earned income: enter type and amount below.	
	Type $ 8a	
	9 Add lines 7 and 8a. These are your **total payments.** 9	1 431 00
	10 **Tax.** Use the amount on **line 6 above** to find your tax in the tax table on pages 24–28 of the booklet. Then, enter the tax from the table on this line. 10	1 289 00
Refund Have it directly deposited! See page 20 and fill in 11b, 11c, and 11d.	11a If line 9 is larger than line 10, subtract line 10 from line 9. This is your **refund.** 11a	
	▶ b Routing number	
	▶ c Type: Checking Savings d Account number	
Amount you owe	12 If line 10 is larger than line 9, subtract line 9 from line 10. This is the **amount you owe.** See page 21 for details on how to pay. 12	

I have read this return. Under penalties of perjury, I declare that to the best of my knowledge and belief, the return is true, correct, and accurately lists all amounts and sources of income I received during the tax year.

Sign here ▶ Your signature | Spouse's signature if joint return. See page 11.

Keep copy for your records. | Date | Your occupation | Date | Spouse's occupation

For Official Use Only

1 2 3 4 5
6 7 8 9 10

May the IRS discuss this return with the preparer shown on back (see page 21)? ☐ Yes ☐ No

Skills Survey

You have seen how useful math is when managing your money. The exercises in this section will help you sharpen your skills.

1. Write the following amounts in words as you would for a check.

   a. $6 _____

   b. $101.50 _____

   c. $58.34 _____

   d. $1,200 _____

2. Add the amounts listed on each deposit slip.

   a.

Date _____	ACCOUNT NUMBER	
Deposit to Account of _____		

	Dollars	Cents
Cash	31	52
Checks 1	109	50
2	342	10
3		
Bank Use only Total		

   b.

Date _____	ACCOUNT NUMBER	
Deposit to Account of _____		

	Dollars	Cents
Cash	185	60
Checks 1	34	75
2	1200	40
3		
Bank Use only Total		

3. Fill in the balance line after each check.

CHECK NO.	DATE	CHECK ISSUED TO OR DESCRIPTION OF DEPOSIT	DEPOSITS AMOUNT	AMOUNT OF CHECK	✓ T	BALANCE	
						1420	75
180	JAN. 1	ALLEN REALTY RENT		250	00		
181	JAN. 15	BANK FOR SAVINGS LOAN		75	50		
182	JAN. 18	GRAND SOUND TV		398	25		

4. What is the total yearly cost of these monthly payments?

   a. **Amount: $225** b. **Amount: $68.13** c. **Amount: $170.35**

   Yearly cost:_____   Yearly cost: _____   Yearly cost:_____

5. What is the monthly rate of interest for each of these loans?

   a. Amount borrowed: $500 for 5 months

      Interest: $50

      Rate of interest: _____

   b. Amount borrowed: $600 for 6 months

      Interest: $36

      Rate of interest: _____

6. How much interest will you pay a year for each loan?

   a. Loan: $550 at 12% a year

      Amount of interest: _____

   b. Loan: $2,250 at $11\frac{1}{2}$% a year

      Amount of interest: _____

On Your Own

A. Banks offer several types of savings plans. Get a brochure from your neighborhood bank and decide which plan is best for you.

B. There are many kinds of insurance—life, fire and theft, automobile collision, credit, etc. Talk to an insurance agent and find out which one might be necessary for you. However, don't let the agent talk you into buying a policy you don't need!

Math Goes to Work

section **4**

Getting the **most money** for the **time you work** means **using math**.

Contents

1. The Best Paying Job 54

2. Working Time. 55

3. Time-and-a-Half. 56

4. Earning by the Piece or by Commission 58

5. What Is Profit? Loss? 59

6. Pricing 61

7. Bookkeeping 62

8. Putting It All Together. 63

   Skills Survey 65

1. The Best Paying Job

Do **help wanted** ads tell you exactly how much you'll make when you get a job? This lesson will help you figure out the take-home pay you can expect from the jobs described in the ads.

PHOTOGRAPHERS
$10.40/hr.
9:30–3:30 p.m., 5 days a wk. Talented people needed for on-location assignments. Write to: Conte's Photos 1475 Queen St. West Toronto, Ontario

FAST FOOD CASHIER TRAINEE
$6.50/hr.
5 days, 9–1 p.m. or 1–5 p.m. Ideal for students and working parents. Will train. Call Benny's Burgers 672-4785.

TRAVEL GUIDE
$8.80/hr.
5 hrs./day, 5 days/wk. Must speak fluent Japanese. J-Tours, 201 E. 50th St., Fifth Fl.

Quick Reference

These abbreviations and terms are important to know:
Hrs./Day = total number of hours worked in 1 day
Days/Wk. = total number of days worked in 1 week
FWT = Federal Withholding Tax
FICA = Social Security Tax under the Federal Insurance Contribution Act
Gross pay = hourly rate x total hours worked
Deductions = total taxes and other payments paid by the employee
Net pay = gross pay – deductions
Taxes withheld usually come from tables provided by the government to employers. Higher gross pay usually means higher percentage of tax deducted.

Fill in the missing amounts on the weekly check stub for each job. Follow the steps used in the example.

1. PHOTOGRAPHER

Hrs./Day	FWT
6	$46.80
Days/Wk.	**FICA**
5	$22.50
Total Hrs.	**State**
30	$16.85
	City
	$10.92
	Other
Rate	
$10.40	**Total Deductions**
Gross Pay	B. $97.07
A. $312.00	**Net Pay**
	C. $214.93
Detach and retain for personal records	

2. FAST FOOD CASHIER TRAINEE

Hrs./Day	FWT
	$19.50
Days/Wk.	**FICA**
	$9.75
Total Hrs.	**State**
	$7.02
	City
	$4.55
	Other
Rate	
$6.50	**Total Deductions**
Gross Pay	B. _____
A. _____	**Net Pay**
	C. _____
Detach and retain for personal records	

3. TRAVEL GUIDE

Hrs./Day	FWT
	$33.00
Days/Wk.	**FICA**
	$16.50
Total Hrs.	**State**
	$11.88
	City
	$7.70
	Other
Rate	
$8.80	**Total Deductions**
Gross Pay	B. _____
A. _____	**Net Pay**
	C. _____
Detach and retain for personal records	

On Your Own

Find the Classified Ad section in your local newspaper. Do you see a job that might fit your interests? Figure out the take-home pay you can expect from the job if deductions are usually 25% of gross pay.

Quick Reference

1 day = 24 hours   1 hour (hr.) = 60 minutes
Any amount of time more than 59 minutes should be changed into hours and minutes by dividing the minutes by 60.

```
      1 hr. 25 min.
60) 85 min.
    60
    25
```

Here are examples of how time is computed:

Adding time:

```
 1 hr. 25 min.                        3 hr.
+2 hr. 55 min.   1 hr. 20 min.      +1 hr. 20 min.
 3 hr. 80 min.   60) 80              4 hr. 20 min.
                    60
                    20
```

Subtracting time:

```
 7 hr. 15 min.  _   6 hr. 75 min.
 5 hr. 45 min.  =  -5 hr. 45 min.
                    1 hr. 30 min.
```

Multiplying time:

```
45 hr. 45 min.                       25 hr.
   x 5          3 hr. 45 min.      + 3 hr. 45 min.
25 hr. 225 min. 60) 225             28 hr. 45 min.
                    180
                     45
```

Dividing time:

```
     5 hr.   9 min.
7) 36 hr. 3 min.
   35
    1 hr. = 60 min.
           63 min.
           63
           00
```

TRY IT!   *Add:*   *Subtract:*
```
            5 hr. 45 min.      8 hr. 25 min.
           +4 hr. 20 min.     - 4 hr. 45 min.
```

            Multiply: *Divide:*
```
            1 hr. 25 min.     5) 21 hr. 15 min.
               x 6
```

What **time** do you arrive at work? **When** do you leave? Your answers could mean **money**! This lesson is all about calculating the amount of time you spend at work.

The following chart shows the amount of time each employee at Pocket Bookstore worked per day. Find the total time for each employee.

	Johnson	Angeles	Brown
MONDAY	7 hr. 30 min.	8 hr. 40 min.	6 hr. 45 min.
WEDNESDAY	5 hr. 45 min.	6 hr. 15 min.	7 hr. 35 min.
FRIDAY	7 hr. 10 min.	5 hr. 50 min.	8 hr. 20 min.
TOTAL TIME			

These employees know how much time they worked on their first day. They want to know how much time they might be able to put in each week. Compute the weekly time for each employee.

	Sherman	Cheng	Perez
TIME IN ONE DAY	8 hr. 10 min.	7 hr. 30 min.	6 hr. 45 min.
NUMBER OF DAYS AT WORK	4	5	6
TOTAL TIME FOR ONE WEEK			

On Your Own

Now you're a time expert. Use your skills to figure out the average time you spend each week on your daily activities, like going to school, playing sports, watching TV, or reading.

3. Time-and-a-Half

How does it feel if your paycheck is larger than you expected? Great! It can happen—if your job pays extra for **overtime**. This lesson will help you understand overtime pay and how it adds up on top of your regular salary.

Examine the earnings of the following employees based on their time cards.

Week Ending __OCTOBER 30__ 20 __02__

S.S. No. __121-44-3003__

Name __CAROL STEINBERG__

		IN	OUT	IN	OUT	IN	OUT	DAILY TOTALS
DAYS								
1	M	8:15	12:00	1:00	4:30			7:15
2	Tu	8:15	12:00	1:00	4:45			7:30
3	W	8:10	12:00	1:15	4:55			7:30
4	Th	8:05	11:55	1:00	4:55			7:45
5	F	8:00	12:00	12:55	5:25			8:30
6	Sa							
7	Su							

		HOURS	RATE	AMOUNT
	REGULAR	35	7.42	A 259.70
	OVERTIME	B $3\frac{1}{2}$	C 11.13	D 38.96

DAYS WORKED	5	TOTAL HOURS	$38\frac{1}{2}$	GROSS EARNINGS	E 298.66

A. Regular pay = $7.42 X 35 = $259.70

B. Overtime = $38\frac{1}{2} - 35 = 3\frac{1}{2}$ OR 3.5 HR.

C. Time-and-a-half rate = $7.42 X 1.5 = $11.13

D. Overtime pay = 3.5 X $11.13 = $38.955 OR $38.96

E. Gross earnings = $259.70 + $38.96 = $298.66

Use what you've learned.

1. Please fill in answers to A–E.

Tip Toe Shoe Shop

Week Ending __MAY 2__ 20 __02__

S.S. No. __095-44-3730__

Name __JACK VARGAS__

	IN	OUT	IN	OUT	IN	OUT	DAILY TOTALS
DAYS 1 M	7:30	12:00	1:10	4:35			7:55
2 Tu	7:20	12:00	1:00	4:55			8:35
3 W	7:25	11:55	1:05	4:25			7:60
4 Th	7:35	11:55	1:10	4:20			7:30
5 F	7:40	11:20	12:30	4:30			7:40
6 Sa							
7 Su							

		HOURS	RATE	AMOUNT
	REGULAR	35	8.50	A
	OVERTIME	B	C	D

DAYS WORKED	5	TOTAL HOURS	39 ½	GROSS EARNINGS	E

A. Regular pay = _____

B. Overtime = _____

C. Time-and-a-half rate = _____

D. Overtime pay = _____

E. Gross earnings = _____

On Your Own

Choose a job that you would like to have. Fill out a time card with the hours that you think you would spend on the job. Include overtime. Look in the newspaper to find an hourly rate for that job. Then figure out the total hours worked per week, your regular pay, overtime pay, and gross earnings.

Week Ending _____ 20 _____

No _____

Name _____

	IN	OUT	IN	OUT	IN	OUT	DAILY TOTALS
DAYS 1 M							
2 Tu							
3 W							
4 Th							
5 F							
6 Sa							
7 Su							

		HOURS	RATE	AMOUNT
	REGULAR			A
	OVERTIME	B	C	D

DAYS WORKED	TOTAL HOURS	GROSS EARNINGS	E

57

4. Earning by the Piece or by Commission

What rewards do you get for working hard? If your pay is based on **the number of items you make** or **sell**, the rewards of hard work are visible: You earn more when you make or sell more!

This lesson will help you understand how piecework earnings and commission on sales are computed.

Read the facts about each person carefully. Then compute his or her earnings.

Quick Reference

Piece rate = amount of money earned on each piece made.

Piecework earnings = piece rate x number of pieces made.

Example: A jewelrymaker earns $2.60 for each piece of jewelry. How much will he or she earn for making 56 pieces?

Piecework earnings = $2.60 x 56

= $145.60

Commission = A percentage of a salesperson's total sales.

Example: Suppose you sell computers at 15% commission. How much will you earn if your total sales amount is $7,500?

Commission = 15% of $7,500

= .15 x 7500

= $1,125

1. Susan makes canvas bags at a piece rate of $1.39. When she makes 95 bags in one week, what is her weekly pay? Susan's earnings =

_____ x _____

= _____

2. Mark makes belts in 3 sizes. The piece rates for each size are: small = $.50, medium = $.75, and large = $1.00. Compute Mark's total earnings on the chart below.

Size	Number of Belts Made	Piece Rate	Earnings
Small	25		
Medium	29		
Large	27		
TOTAL			

3. Elena Carlos sold a house for $145,000. If her commission is 5%, how much did she earn? Elena's Commission =

_____ % of $ _____

= _____ x _____

= $ _____

4. Suppose you earn $1.16 for each record that you sell for $14.50. What percent commission are you being paid?

Percent commission = $\dfrac{\text{Earnings}}{\text{Sales}}$ x 100

= $\dfrac{\$1.16}{14.50}$ x 100 $14.50\overline{)116.00}$ with $.06$

= _____ x _____

= _____ %

On Your Own

You have seen many different ways of earning. Choose 3 different jobs described in the previous pages. Then compute the earnings for each job. What are the benefits of each? What is the downside of each? Which one would you rather have? Why?

5. What Is Profit? Loss?

When you buy a pair of skates for $10 and sell them for $15, your profit is $5. But suppose you spend $7 on classified ads before you sell the skates? Then you have a loss of $2! This lesson will help you understand profit and loss when running a business.

Read the following facts and then answer the questions.

1. The skateboard that you bought for $12 was sold for $14.50. What was your gross profit? _____

2. You bought a plain T-shirt for $3.99. The iron-on letters that you put on the shirt cost you $2.50. How much should you sell the T-shirt for to earn a profit of $4?

   Cost of plain T-shirt = _____

   Additional cost of
   letters   + _____

   Cost of T-shirt   = _____

   Profit   + _____

   Selling price   = _____

> ### Quick Reference
>
> **Total sales** = the sum of the amounts you receive from customers.
>
> **Cost of goods sold** = the amount you paid for the things you sell.
>
> **Gross profit** = Total sales minus cost of goods sold.
>
> **Operating expenses** = the sum of amounts paid for doing business (rent, utilities, telephone, office supplies, salaries, advertising, and others).
>
> **Net profit** = Gross profit minus operating expenses.
>
> **Net loss** = the difference between gross profit and operating expenses, if the expense amount is greater than the profit.
>
> **Unit cost** = the amount you paid for one of the items you sell.
>
> **Inventory** = number of goods for sale x unit cost.

3. When you tried to sell the T-shirt at your selling price, nobody wanted to buy it! So you sold it for $5.

   Did you have a profit? A loss?

   Cost of T-shirt for sale _____

   Amount paid to you _____

   Difference _____

   Is this a profit or a loss? _____

CANDLELIGHT SHOPPE
Profit and Loss Statement for the Month of May

TOTAL SALES		$ ....A
COSTS:		
May 1 inventory	$ ....B	
New purchases	+ C	
Total cost of candles for sale	..............D	
May 31 inventory	– ....E	
COST OF GOODS SOLD	....	$ ....F
GROSS PROFIT	....	$............G
EXPENSES		
....	$	
....	....	} H
....	....	
TOTAL OPERATING EXPENSES	....	$ I
NET PROFIT (or LOSS)	....	$ ....J

Prepare a PROFIT & LOSS STATEMENT for this business. Read the facts for each letter carefully.

A. The weekly sales in May were:

First week:	$155.50
Second week:	186.75
Third week:	195.00
Fourth week:	175.25
TOTAL SALES	

B. On May 1, there were 1,500 candles in the store and each candle cost $.05.

1500 x .05 = _____

C. The new candles bought in May cost $200.

D. Add B and C.

E. On May 31, there were 2,000 candles in the store at $.05 each.

2000 x .05 = _____

F. Subtract E from D.

G. Subtract F from A.

H. To run the store, the owner paid $200 rent, $100 for ads and $95 for supplies.

I. Add the amounts in H.

J. Subtract I from G.

Note: If expenses are greater than the gross profit, the difference is a LOSS.

On Your Own

Suppose you want to earn money by making models of spaceships, submarines, or unusual cars. Find out how much the materials will cost. Don't forget to add the cost of your labor! Figure your hourly rate and multiply it by the number of hours you might spend on a model. Your selling price should include the total cost of your materials and your labor, plus some profit.

Quick Reference

Unit cost is the amount you pay for one item.

Mark-up is the amount added to the unit cost to find the **selling price**. Mark-up is usually a percentage of the unit cost. The mark-up helps to cover operating expenses and to generate profit.

The selling price of a skateboard with a unit cost of $9.80 and a 25% mark-up is computed this way:

Mark-up = 25% of $9.80
= .25 x $9.80
= $2.45

Selling price =
Cost of item + mark-up
= $9.80
+ $2.45
= $12.25

When you buy a stamp collection for $10 and sell it for $11, are you really making money? Perhaps not! The price may not be enough to cover the cost of operating your business. This lesson will help you understand pricing of goods for sale.

Read the facts carefully and answer the questions.

1. Suppose you build model spaceships and sell them for a profit. The materials for one model cost $2.50. To pay for your labor and other expenses, you must price your models with a 400% mark-up on cost. What is the selling price of one model spaceship?

Mark-up = $ _____ x _____

= _____ x _____ %

= _____

Selling price = $ _____ + $ _____

= $ _____

2. Lower prices often invite more sales. If your prices are higher than most stores, you may not be able to sell your goods. The following chart shows how the lower mark-up affected the total sales of a calculator. Find the missing mark-ups and totals.

Cost	% Mark-up	Mark-up	Total Number of Calculators Sold	Total Mark-up or Gross Profit
$12.00	20%	$2.40	200	
$12.00	25%		175	
$12.00	30%		100	
$12.00	35%		50	

Which mark-up had the highest gross profit?

_____

7. Bookkeeping

How's business? Your answer depends on what your **records** show. This lesson is all about keeping up-to-date records of your business activities.

1.

DATE		EXPLANATION	RECEIVED		PAID OUT		BALANCE	
June	1	Balance brought forward	545	60			545	60
June	5	New Sweaters			210	00		
June	5	Sales	501	95				
June	12	Sales	750	00				
June	14	Paper Supplies			22	80		
June	15	Express Realty			250	00		
June	19	Sales	620	50				

This is a **cash record**. It looks similar to a check register. Fill in each missing balance by adding amounts received and subtracting amounts paid out.

2. This is a **sales report**. You use it to find total sales and to keep track of which items sell the most and the least. Fill in the missing totals per week in the right column and the totals per item along the bottom.

Sales Report

WEEK ENDING	DEPARTMENTS			TOTAL
	SWEATERS	VESTS	BLOUSES	
June 5	$200.95	$61.50	$40.50	
June 12	$325.25	$170.50	$54.25	
June 19	$237.80	$180.30	$202.40	
June 26	$420.00	$215.60	$208.70	
TOTAL				

3.

DATE	PAYEE	AMOUNT PAID	SWEATERS	VESTS	MIXED BLOUSES
June 1	Sweaters, Inc.	210.00	210.00		
June 23	Tops, Co.	195.20			195.20
June 25	Best of Vests, Inc.	88.95		88.95	
June 28	Mixed Blouses, Inc.	54.25			54.25
June 29	Vests, Inc.	90.00		90.00	
June 30	Sweaters, Unlimited	77.50	77.50		
	TOTAL				

This is a **record of purchases**. It shows the date, payee (person or company paid), and the amount paid for items purchased. This record is helpful when you want to know the cost of inventory. Fill in the missing totals along the bottom.

4. This is a **record of operating expenses**. It is a detailed picture of how much it costs you to run your business. The report includes the date, payee, amount paid, and what you paid for. Fill in the missing entries and totals.

DATE	PAYEE	AMOUNT PAID	ADS	PHONE UTILITIES	SUPPLIES	OTHER
June 15	Express Realty	250.00		250.00		
June 20	Paper Bag Co.	55.40			55.40	
June 22	Times	60	60.00			
June 25	Bell Telephone	15.40				
June 27	Bus Co.	25.50				
June 30	Advertising Limited	50.00				
	TOTAL					

1. Compute the gross pay, total deductions, and net pay on this check stub.

Hr./Day	FWT
7	$44.27
Days/Wk.	FICA
5	$33.67
Total Hrs.	State
35	$45.28
	City
	$2.42
	Other
Rate	.60
$15.90	Total Deductions
Gross Pay	
	Net Pay

Detach and retain for personal records.

2. Stella works 2 days each week. First compute her total hours in the office for one week. Next, subtract the coffee breaks and lunch breaks. Find the total hours she might work in 4 weeks. Then compute her average.

Tuesday   5 hr. 45 min.
Thursday   +8 hr. 30 min.
1 Wk. Total   hr.   min.

Breaks   −1 hr. 45 min.
Actual time   hr.   min.

Total in 4 weeks   x 4 weeks
                        hr.   min.

Average time per day =   Total in 4 wks.
                          Number of days
                          worked in 4 wks.

What is Stella's average? ____hr. _____min.

3. Here is part of a time card.

		HOURS	RATE	AMOUNT
	REGULAR	35	$6	
	OVERTIME			
DAYS WORKED 6	TOTAL HOURS	42	GROSS EARNINGS	

Fill in with the following:

A. Overtime hours

B. Time-and-a-half rate

C. Regular pay

D. Overtime pay

E. Gross earnings

4. a. Jim earns $.05 for each newspaper he delivers. How much does he make after delivering 50 newspapers?

   _____

   b. Barbara earns 6% commission for each TV she sells. If a TV costs $399, how much commission does she earn?

   _____

5. a. Suppose you bought a radio for $15 and sold it for $25. What was your gross profit?

   _____

   b. To sell the radio, you spent $4 for ads. What was your net profit?

   _____

Putting It All Together

Due to space limitations, the answers to questions 6 and 7 do not appear in the answer key.

6. In order to pay for operating cost and to have some net profit, a photographer must take pictures with a 85% mark-up on cost. What should be the selling price for each of the following sizes of pictures?

Size	Cost	85% Mark-up on Cost	Selling Price
$2 \frac{1}{2}$ X $2 \frac{1}{2}$	$.60		
5 X 7	1.20		
8 X 10	2.40		

7. Fill out this cash record with the following information:

May 1: The balance brought forward is $500.

May 2: You paid $250 rent.

May 4: You received $150 from sales.

May 6: You paid *Times* $65 for ads.

DATE	EXPLANATION	RECEIVED	PAID OUT	BALANCE

1. Add.

```
  13.50
   6.18
   3.10
   1.25                1 hr. 15 min.        7 hr. 20 min.
a.  + .60        b. +3 hr. 10 min.    c. +1 hr. 55 min.
```
d. 27.90 + 11.69 + 6.60 + 2.90 + .90 = _____

2. Subtract.

```
   $1575.40          $1113.00        3 hr. 50 min.      2 hr. 10 min.
a.  −342.20     b.  −435.67     c. −1 hr. 45      d. −1 hr. 25 min.
                                      min.
```
e. $198.50 − $52.92 = _____

3. Multiply.

```
   $15.50                3.50 x .25 =        3 hr. 10 min.       4 hr. 35 min.
a.   x 35       b.  4.20 x 1  =       c.  ___ x 3 ___     d.  ___ x 4 ___
```

4. Divide.

a. 70$\overline{)145.60}$ **b.** 1/5 =   **c.** 3$\overline{)9\ \text{hr. 6 min.}}$ **d.** 2$\overline{)3\ \text{hr. 12 min.}}$ **e.** 10.60 ÷ 530 = _____

5. Compute these percentages.

a. 500% of $3 = _____

b. 6% of $450 = _____

c. 25% of $184 = _____

d. 350% of $.36 = _____

e. 8% of $.84 = _____

f. 1.5% of $23 = _____

On Your Own

A. Interview one or two people who own a business. Ask them what they like or don't like about being on their own.

B. Find out the difference between wholesale price and retail price. How much discount do stores usually get from wholesalers?

Math Savers

section **5**

Math can help you fight rising costs and spend your money more **wisely**.

Contents

1. City and Highway Mileage 67

2. Gas Saving Habits 69

3. Do It Yourself 70

4. Using the Calculator's Memory 71

5. Discounts 73

6. Buy More, Pay Less 74

7. Putting It All Together 75

   Skills Survey 76

1. City and Highway Mileage

Quick Reference

MPG means miles per gallon, or the number of miles you can travel on one gallon of gas. This number can be different if you're driving on a highway or in a city.

To compute number of gallons used in the city:

- Divide total city miles driven by the city MPG.
- Round your answer to the second decimal place.

To compute number of gallons used on the highway:

- Divide total miles driven on highway by the highway MPG.
- Round your answer to the nearest tens.

To compute total gallons used by your car:

- Add gallons used in city to gallons used on highway.

What goes up when the other goes down? Gasoline cost and car mileage! Because of rising gasoline costs, car makers are forced to produce cars that use less gasoline for each mile traveled. This lesson will help you understand mileage and how it affects the cost of operating a car.

The cars listed on the chart below were tested on city roads and on highways. Each column shows the number of miles traveled by each car using one gallon of gasoline. Use the chart below to answer questions 1–3 on page 68.

CAR MILEAGE CHART		
	City MPG	Hwy. MPG
BMW 5 series	18	26
VW New Beetle	24	31
Cadillac DeVille	17	28
Range Rover	13	16
Lexus GS300	19	25
Mercedes SUV	15	19
Nissan Frontier	20	24
Saturn SC	27	38
Toyota Camry Solara	20	28
Ford Windstar Minivan	17	23

1. Three people driving different cars travel 50 city miles and 200 highway miles in a week. How many gallons of gas will each driver use?

   a. The BMW Driver

City	Highway	Total Gallons Used

   b. The Lexus Driver

City	Highway	Total Gallons Used

   c. The Cadillac Driver

City	Highway	Total Gallons Used

2. Suppose the same drivers in question 1 drive 200 city miles and 50 highway miles in a week. How many gallons of gas will each driver use?

	City	Highway	Total Gallons Used
a. BMW			
b. Lexus			
c. Cadillac			

3. Four commuters using different cars drive 120 city miles and 250 highway miles each week. If a gallon of gas costs $1.55, what is the weekly cost of gasoline for each car listed below? Use the chart on the opposite page for MPG for each car.

Type of Car Driven	Gas Used in City	Gas Used on Highway	Total Gas Used a Week	Weekly Cost
a. VW				
b. Nissan				
c. Ford Windstar				
d. Mercedes				

■ ■

On Your Own

Choose a car that you would like to buy. Find out how many miles per gallon it can travel in the city and on the highway. Set up your own commuting plan and figure your gasoline cost per week.

2. Gas Saving Habits

So you like fast starts and high speeds? Here's news for you—you're a gas guzzler. Your car may have been advertised with a mileage rate of 30 miles per gallon, but your driving habits can easily pull the mileage down to 15 MPG. This lesson is all about improving your driving habits and computing savings on gas.

The bar graph at right shows you that for the same distance traveled, your car's gasoline consumption increases as you increase speed. Use the graph to answer questions 1–4.

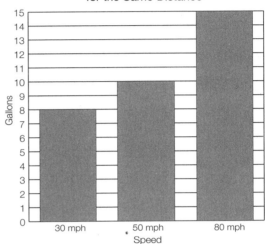

Gasoline Used at Different Speeds for the Same Distance

1. a. 8 gallons of gas were used to drive 250 miles at 30 mph (miles per hour). How many gallons were used at 50 mph? _____

   How many gallons were used at 80 mph?

   _____

   b. If gas is $1.43 per gallon, how much more did it cost to drive 50 mph? 80 mph? _____

2. Suppose your car travels 45 miles at 50 mph and uses 2 gallons of gas. How many miles per gallon can it travel at this speed?_____

3. At 80 mph your car will use 3 gallons of gas for the same 45 miles. What is your car's MPG at this speed? _____

4. Mark's car uses 4 gallons of gas to travel 120 miles at 30 mph. At 50 mph, the car uses 5 gallons of gas and at 80 mph, the amount of gas used increases to $7\frac{1}{2}$ gallons. If gasoline costs $1.60 per gallon, what is the total cost of gasoline used at each speed?

MPH	Number of Gallons Used	Total Cost of Gasoline

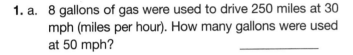

On Your Own

Ask an automobile salesperson what effects these additional accessories have on gasoline mileage:

A. An 8-cylinder rather than a 6-cylinder engine
B. air-conditioning,
C. automatic transmission,
D. power brakes, power steering, power doors and windows.

Quick Reference

Gas-saving habits:

- Avoid fast starts and stops. Drive at reduced speeds.
- When parked, turn off the engine. A car idling for six minutes uses as much gasoline as driving 1 mile at 30 mph.
- Keep your car in good running condition. Have it checked regularly.
- By driving sensibly and keeping your car in good shape, you can save at least 15% on gasoline costs.

Use the Quick Reference Box to answer questions 5 and 6.

5. On a trip to Toronto from New York, Mr. Johnson drove through downtown Buffalo instead of taking the bypass around it. Because of heavy traffic, his car was stopped with the motor running for at least 12 minutes. Mr. Johnson wasted as much gasoline as driving _____ miles at _____ mph.

6. Sandy Lightfoot figured out that by driving sensibly and keeping her car in good shape, she reduced the cost of driving her car by $.025 per mile. How much savings is this if she drives 12,850 miles a year?

3. Do It Yourself

More and more people are decorating their homes and doing minor repairs themselves. This lesson will help you understand how to **measure area** in your home so that you can decorate it yourself.

Use the Quick Reference box and the ad below to answer questions 1 and 2.

1. Find the area in sq. ft. of each room in this floor plan.

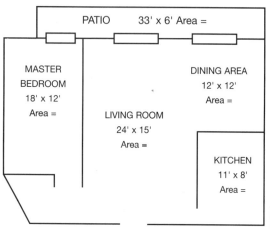

PATIO   33' x 6' Area =

MASTER BEDROOM
18' x 12'
Area =

DINING AREA
12' x 12'
Area =

LIVING ROOM
24' x 15'
Area =

KITCHEN
11' x 8'
Area =

2. Fill in the chart below with the facts from the floor plan in question 1. How much will you save if you installed the carpet for each room in question 1 yourself? The patio is done for you.

	Living Room	Bedroom	Dining Room	Patio	
Length in Yd.				11 YD.	
Width in Yd.				2 YD.	
Area in Sq. Yd.				22 SQ. YD.	
Price per Sq. Yd.	$13.95	$11.95	$10.95	$9.95	
Installation Charge per Sq. Yd.	3.99	3.99	3.99	3.99	
Total Cost if Installed				$306.68	— 22 SQ. YD. X (9.95 +3
Total Cost if You Install Yourself				$218.90	— 22 SQ. YD. X 9.95
Do-It-Yourself Savings				$87.78	— 306.68 – 218.90

Due to space limitations, these answers do not appear in the answer key.

On Your Own

A. Find the area of the living room, dining area, and kitchen in square centimeters and in square meters.

B. Take the measurements of your room. How many square yards of carpet would it need? How many square inches of 8" x 8" tiles?

LIVING ROOM
7 m x 4 m
Area =

DINING AREA
3 m x 2 m
Area =

KITCHEN
4 m x 2 m
Area =

4. Using the Calculator's Memory

Often, solving real-life problems takes more than one step. That's when the **calculator's memory** comes in handy. This lesson will show you how to use your calculator and its memory to solve some day-to-day problems. For a beginning lesson on using the calculator, please turn to page 21.

please turn to page 21.

Quick Reference

MR = Memory recall—shows what's in the memory

M– = Remember and subtract

M+ = Remember and add

C = If you press the wrong number key, just press C to correct the error. If you press the wrong operation key, just press the correct one and continue.

√ = Square root

% = Percent

When you work with money, set calculator at (2) and all decimals will be rounded to 2 places.

The following examples show you how problems are solved with a calculator.

1. A $58 coat is on sale at 25% off. Find the discount and the discount price.

   Press these calculator keys, in order:

   [AC] [5] [8] [X] [2] [5] [%]   Read-out: **14.50**

   Then press: [–]   Read-out: **43.50**

The discount is $14.50. (Some calculators may not show the last zero. The read-out would show 14.5.) The discount price is $43.50.

2. A $35 dress is on sale at 15% off. An $18 sweater is on sale at 10% off. How much would you pay for the two items? Press these calculator keys in order:

   [AC] [3] [5] [X] [1] [5] [%] [–] [M+]   Read-out: **29.75**

   [1] [8] [X] [1] [0] [%] [–] [M+]   Read-out: **16.20**

   [MR]   Read-out: **45.95**

Due to space limitations, the answers to these questions do not appear in the answer key.

3. Fill in the missing numbers.

Cost $50	`AC` `5` `0`	Cost $89	`AC` `8` `9`	Bill $12.99	`AC` `1` `2` `•` `9` `9`
% off 10%	`X` `•` `1` `0`	Mark-up 15%	`X` `•` `1` `5`	Sales Tax 8%	`X` `•` ☐ ☐ ☐
Discount	☐ ☐ ☐	Mark-up	☐ ☐ ☐	Tax	☐ ☐ ☐ ☐
Sale Price	☐ ☐ `–`	Selling Price	☐ ☐ `+`	Total	`+` ☐ ☐ ☐

4. Find the total cost.

Shoes $45, 10% off `AC` `4` `5` `X` `•` `1` `0` `–` `M+` _____

Socks $1.55, 5% off `1` `•` `5` `5` `X` `•` `0` `5` `–` `M+` _____

Slacks $17.99, 15% off `1` `7` `•` `9` `9` `X` `•` `1` `5` `–` `M+` _____

Shirt $10.50, 10% off `1` `0` `•` `5` `0` `X` `•` `1` `0` `–` `M+` _____

Total `MR` _____

5. Check the sales slips to see that the totals are correct. The first one is done for you.

				1.10
			.45	1.10
	`AC`		.45	.55
8.55	`8` `•` `5` `5` `M+`	1.19	.45	.55
.39	`•` `3` `9` `M+`	2.25	.79	6.52
.39	`M+`	.71	.79	.15
.39	`M+`	.89	1.08	.15
1.25	`1` `•` `2` `5` `M+`	1.09	2.16	.15
1.25	`M+`	3.99	1.12	2.08
Total 12.22	`MR`	Total 10.83	Total 7.29	Total 12.35

_____   _____   _____

5. Discounts

SALE!

50% off on entire summer stock

20% off on items marked with ✱

15% off on all other items

You heard about the storewide sale and came prepared with a shopping list. But, how much will you really save on each item? This lesson will help you find the amount of **discount** and the new sale price from given percentages.

Use the ad at left to determine the percentage of discount for each item listed. Then compute the amount of discount and the discounted price.

Due to space limitations, the answers to these questions do not appear in the answer key.

Item	Price	% of Discount	Amount of Discount in Dollars & Cents	Discounted Price
Swimsuit	$23.99			
Sleeveless Dress	27.50			
Bathing Cap	3.65			
Sandals	19.99			
Jacket*	34.25			
Mittens*	7.69			
Raincoat*	18.35			
Boots	45.68			
Sweater	26.89			
Coat	63.30			

Total _____   Total _____

Quick Reference

To compute the amount of discount:

- Multiply the percentage (in decimal form) by the original selling price.
- Round to the second decimal place.

To compute the new discounted price:

- Subtract amount of discount from original selling price.

Three people bought the same type of coat in different stores. Find the discounted price of the coat in each store.

In which store was the coat cheapest? _____

Store	Price Tag	% of Discount	Amount of Discount	Sale Price
Honi's	$69.95	20%		
Stella's	$79.60	25%		
Rachel's	$59.80	15%		

On Your Own

Look for advertised sales in the newspaper. List the things you would like to buy and figure out the discounted price from the advertised percentages.

Item	Sale Price
_____	_____
_____	_____
_____	_____

73

6. Buy More, Pay Less

How can you **pay less** when you **buy more**? This lesson will help you find out how you can sometimes save money by buying more of an item.

Read the facts in questions 1–5 carefully. Decide if you pay less by buying more.

1. One bar of soap costs $.64. A three-bar pack costs $1.90. How much money do you save by buying the three-bar pack instead of three separate bars?

   _____

2. A 16 oz. bottle of shampoo costs $3.28. An 8 oz. bottle costs $1.74. How much money do you save by buying the larger bottle instead of two small bottles?

   _____

3. A 10-pound bag of rice costs $3.98. You can buy smaller bags in the following amounts:

   1-pound bag—$.49   2-pound bag—$.91

   5-pound bag—$2.15

   How much would 10 pounds of rice cost if you buy it in:

   a. 1-pound bags?   _____

   b. 2-pound bags?   _____

   c. 5-pound bags?   _____

   How much do you save by buying the 10-pound bag instead of:

   d. 1-pound bags?   _____

   e. 2-pound bags?   _____

   f. 5-pound bags?   _____

4. A two-liter bottle of juice costs $2.59. One liter costs $1.79. Do you save money by buying the larger container?   _____

On Your Own

A tour package includes transportation and hotel expenses. Call a travel agent and find out how much you can save by buying a tour package to Europe instead of getting transportation tickets and hotel accommodations separately.

Quick Reference

Unit price is the amount you pay for one item.

To compute the unit price of one item in a package:

Divide the package price by the number of items in the package.

Example: What is the price of each can in a case of 24 cans that costs $16.80?

$$\text{Unit price} = \begin{array}{r} .70 \\ 24\overline{)16.80} \\ \underline{168} \\ 0 \end{array}$$

Unit price = $.70

To find the total cost of the same number of cans bought separately at $.76 each:

Total cost of 24 cans = $.76 x 24

= $18.24

To find the amount saved by buying the case, instead of separate cans:

$18.24 Total cost of items bought separately

−16.80 Case price

  1.44 Amount saved

5. Read this ad.

a. How much do you save by buying the picnic kit instead of buying the items separately?

   _____

b. Suppose you don't need charcoal. Will you still buy the kit or buy the items separately?

   _____

c. You only need an ice bucket, a thermos bottle, and a barbecue mitt. Will you buy the whole kit or buy the items separately?

   _____

THE PICNIC KIT!
ONLY $19.99!

*If bought separately the items in the kit
will cost as follows:*

Ice bucket	$6.99
Thermos bottle	$8.50
Barbecue mitt	$4.99
Charcoal	$1.69
Skewers	$3.85

1. Three people driving different cars travel 30 city miles and 40 highway miles a day. How many gallons of gasoline are used a day by each driver? Round your answer to the nearest tenth.

	Saab	Honda	Kia
City MPG	17	18	19
Highway MPG	22	26	27
City Gasoline			
Highway Gasoline			
Total			

2. If one gallon of gasoline costs $1.45, how much would the Kia driver in question 1 spend on gasoline each day?

_____

3. Your car uses 2 gallons of gasoline to travel a distance of 48 miles at 50 miles per hour. How many miles can it travel per gallon?

_____

4. If your car used 3 gallons of gas to cover the same 48 miles at 80 mph, what is your car's mileage rate (MPG) at this speed?

_____

5. Find the area in sq. yd. of each room in this floor plan.

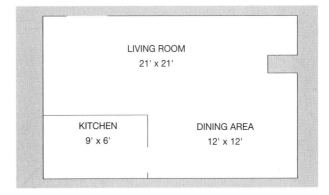

Living Room: Area = _____ sq. yd.

Dining Area: Area = _____ sq. yd.

Kitchen: Area = _____ sq. yd.

6. Three people bought the same style suit in three different stores. Find the discounted price of the suit in each store.

Store	Price	% Discount	Amount of Discount	Sale Price
Jim's	$179.50	33%		
Pat's	$162.80	25%		
Len's	$149.95	20%		

7. Read the ad carefully. Then answer the questions.

BUY MORE, SAVE MORE

FRUIT JUICE
1 case $18.50
24 12-oz. bottles

6-pack $5.40
6 12-oz. bottles

1 12-oz. bottle $1.10

a. What is the unit cost of 1 bottle in a case? _____

b. What is the unit cost of 1 bottle in a 6-pack? _____

c. How much do you save by buying a case instead of buying 24 separate bottles?

_____

Skills Survey

1. Divide the miles driven by the car's MPG to get the total amount of gasoline used.

	Beetle	Camry	Range Rover	Saturn
Miles driven	1116	1708	1210	1350
MPG	31	28	22	27
Amount of gasoline used				

2. Change to yards.

   a. 33 ft. = _____

   b. 45 ft. = _____

   c. 57 ft. = _____

3. Change to inches.

   a. 18 ft. = _____

   b. 12 ft. = _____

   c. 21 ft. = _____

4. Change to feet.

   a. 96 in. = _____

   b. 144 in = _____

   c. 276 in. = _____

5. What is the area of the following rooms?

   a. Bedroom, 12 ft. x 9 ft. _____

   b. Patio, 5 m x 2 m _____

   c. Walk-in closet, 48 in. x 56 in. _____

6. Find the percentages. Round your answer to the nearest penny.

   a. 25% of $45.37 = _____

   b. 33% of $78.50 = _____

   c. 20% of $185 = _____

7. What is the price of 1 bottle in a package of 6 bottles for $3.78?

   _____

8. Which is a better value, 2 for $.99 or 1 for $.50?

   _____

9. A two-liter can of fruit costs $2.79 and a one-liter can costs $1.43. How much money do you save by buying the bigger can?

   _____

On Your Own

Create a shopping list for a dinner party. First, decide how many people will attend, and what you will serve. Next, go to your local super maket and figure out how much the food for your party would cost. Is it less expensive to buy exactly the estimated amount, or to purchase larger, value-size packages?

Math Where You Least Expect It

Even when you're away from work and bills, you're **using your math skills**.

Contents

1. Where Does Your Team Stand? 78

2. Going Places 79

3. Temperature Change . . . . : . 81

4. The Metric System 83

5. Shopping With Foreign Money 85

6. Putting It All Together 87

   Skills Survey 88

1. Where Does Your Team Stand?

Sports news is filled with statistics: records to be broken, number of wins and losses, team standings. You too can **compute the statistics** related to your favorite sports team. This lesson will help you understand how to determine team standings.

Complete the Pct. (percent) column. We did the first one for you.

Quick Reference

W = number of games won   **L** = number of games lost

Pct. = percent of games won (expressed as a decimal)

The team with the highest pct. is considered first in the standings. To compute the pct. of each team:

1. Add the wins and losses to find the total number of games played.

   28 W + 11 L = 39 games

2. Divide the number of games won by the total number of games played. Round your answer to three decimal places.

$$.7179 = .718$$

$$
\begin{array}{r}
39\overline{)28.0000} \\
\underline{27\ 3} \\
70 \\
\underline{39} \\
310 \\
\underline{273} \\
370 \\
\underline{351} \\
19
\end{array}
$$

BASKETBALL TEAM STANDINGS				BASKETBALL TEAM STANDINGS				BASKETBALL TEAM STANDINGS			
Atlantic	**W**	**L**	**Pct.**	Atlanta	19	23		Detroit	17	22	
Philadelphia	28	11	.718	New Orleans	16	24		Kansas City	15	27	
Knicks	22	18		Houston	15	25		**Pacific**	**W**	**L**	**Pct.**
Buffalo	16	22		**Midwest**	**W**	**L**	**Pct.**	Los Angeles	17	24	
Nets	9	32		Denver	27	13		Seattle	22	20	
Central	**W**	**L**	**Pct.**	Chicago	22	19		Portland	32	6	
Washington	24	16		Milwaukee	23	21		Golden State	19	21	
San Antonio	23	18		Indiana	17	21		Phoenix	26	14	
Cleveland	19	19									

Use the basketball team standings above to answer the following questions.

1. Which team has the highest percentage of wins? _____

2. Which team should be higher in the standings: Indiana, Detroit, or Los Angeles? _____

3. Which team has a lower percentage of wins: Seattle or Milwaukee? _____

4. Name the team that has the lowest percentage of wins. _____

5. Place the teams in the Pacific Division in order by putting the best percentage record first.

   a._____   d._____

   b._____   e._____

   c._____

On Your Own

Use the Won/Lost columns for these baseball teams to determine team standings. Arrange the teams in order by placing the one with the best percentage record first. (Round each pct. to three decimal places.)

	W	L	
Twins	97	65	_____
A's	94	68	_____
Royals	90	72	_____
Orioles	91	71	_____
Tigers	86	70	_____
Red Sox	95	65	_____
Yankees	97	62	_____

Look in the sports section of your newspaper. Where else do you see percentages?

Quick Reference

HOW FAR?

Distance (miles or kilometers) = speed x time

HOW FAST?

Speed or rate (miles per hour or kilometers per hour) = $\dfrac{\text{distance}}{\text{time}}$

HOW MUCH TIME?

Time (hours) = $\dfrac{\text{distance}}{\text{speed}}$

1 mile = 1.609 kilometers

1 kilometer = .625 mile

How **far** are you going? How **fast**? How **much time** do you need to get there?

These are some of the questions this lesson will help you to answer.

Use the Quick Reference Box and the road map to answer questions 1–7.

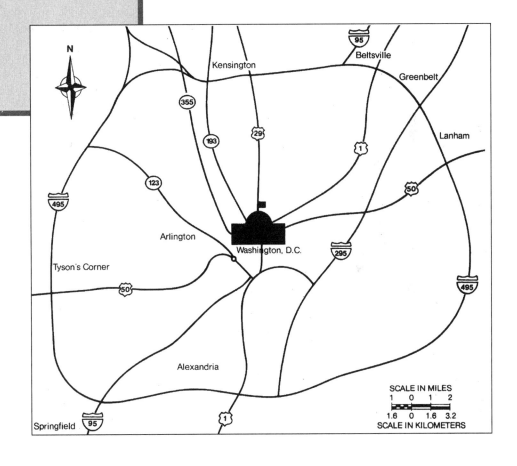

1. Suppose you are on your way to Springfield from Greenbelt. You want to take Route 495 in order to avoid Washington, D.C. You can go southeast through Lanham or southwest through Tyson's Corner. Look at the map. Which way is shorter?

    _____

2. Coming from Greenbelt on your way to Alexandria, you have a choice between Routes 495 and 295. If you take Route 495, you travel a distance of 27 miles at 55 mph (miles per hour). On Route 295 the distance is 20 miles, but the speed limit is 45 mph. Which route will take less time?

    _____

3. The Arlington National Cemetery is about 29 km (kilometers) from Springfield. It takes you $\frac{1}{2}$ hour to get there. How fast are you going?

_____

4. You circled the Washington, D.C., area along Route 495 at 80 km/h (kilometers per hour) for $1\frac{1}{4}$ hour. About how much distance did you cover?

_____

5. From Kensington to downtown Washington, D.C., you have a choice between Route 355 and Route 193. If you take Route 355, you will travel 19 km in 15 minutes or $\frac{1}{4}$ hour. How fast are you going?

_____

6. If you take Route 193, you will travel 10 miles in 30 minutes or $\frac{1}{2}$ hour. How fast are you going?

_____

7. Which route do you think has more traffic problems, 193 or 355?

_____

On Your Own

A. Suppose you're visiting California. You want to drive from Los Angeles to the cities listed on the chart. Fill in the chart with the missing distance, travel time, or average speed.

B. Get a mileage table from the bookstore or library. Calculate distance and travel time for trips to different places you'd like to visit. Compare using different average speeds.

From Los Angeles to:	Distance	Travel Time	Average Speed
San Francisco, Calif.	284 m	6 hr.	
San Diego, Calif.	195 km		65 km/h
Las Vegas, Nev.		5 hr.	57 mph

Is it warm or cool? In the United States, temperature is expressed in degrees Fahrenheit (°F). Many other countries give temperature in degrees Celsius (°C). This lesson will show you how to change from one to the other.

Read the facts in questions 1–8 on page 82, then answer the questions. Round your answers to the nearest whole numbers.

Quick Reference

To convert from Fahrenheit to Celsius:
  Subtract 32.
  Multiply by 5.
  Divide by 9.

To convert from Celsius to Fahrenheit:
  Multiply by 9.
  Divide by 5.
  Add 32.

Convert 50° Fahrenheit to °Celsius.

$$\begin{array}{r} 50 \\ -32 \\ \hline 18 \end{array}$$

$$\begin{array}{r} 18 \\ \times 5 \\ \hline 90 \end{array}$$

$$\begin{array}{r} 10 \\ 9 \overline{)90} \\ \underline{9} \\ 0 \end{array}$$

50°F = 10°C

Convert 10° Celsius to °Fahrenheit.

$$\begin{array}{r} 20 \\ \times 9 \\ \hline 180 \end{array}$$

$$\begin{array}{r} 36 \\ 5 \overline{)180} \\ \underline{15} \\ 30 \\ \underline{30} \\ 0 \end{array}$$

$$\begin{array}{r} 36 \\ +32 \\ \hline 68 \end{array}$$

20°C = 68°F

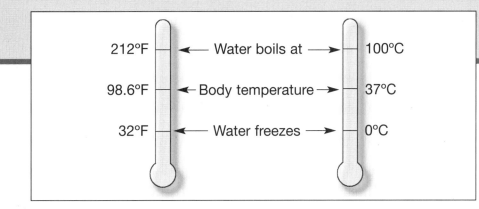

212°F	← Water boils at →	100°C
98.6°F	← Body temperature →	37°C
32°F	← Water freezes →	0°C

1. Celia Carlos of Toronto, Canada, is planning to visit these cities in the United States. She can decide what clothes to bring if the temperatures shown on the chart are expressed in degrees Celsius. Convert the temperatures for Celia.

City	Degrees Fahrenheit	Degrees Celsius
Anchorage	32	
Miami	77	
Phoenix	86	
Seattle	41	
Wichita	59	

2. Scott Jackson of Topeka, Kansas, is traveling around the world in April. In every city he visits the temperature is given in degrees Celsius. Convert the temperatures to degrees Fahrenheit for Scott.

City	Degrees Celsius	Degrees Fahrenheit
Athens	15	
Bangkok	35	
Copenhagen	5	
Peking	11	
Rome	18	

3. You set the thermostat in your house at 34°C. Do you feel comfortable? _____

4. Your body temperature is 40°C. Do you have a fever? _____

5. It is 27°C in Montreal and 72°F in New York. Which is warmer? _____

6. The temperature in Chicago is 33°F and in Vancouver it is 3°C. Which is colder? _____

7. If −10°C means 10 degrees below 0° Celsius, how would you write five degrees below 0° Fahrenheit?

8. What is the Celsius equivalent of 23°F? _____

On Your Own

List the cities you would like to visit this summer. Find out what the temperature will be from an almanac or travel section of the newspaper. Express the temperature in both Fahrenheit and Celsius.

City	Degrees Fahrenheit	Degrees Celsius

Meter, liter, and gram—these are the basic units of length, capacity (volume), and mass (weight) used in the metric system, the measurement language based on 10. It is a decimal system using many standard prefixes, as shown on the chart below. Each prefix has 10 times the value of its neighbor to the right.

Metric Prefixes

Prefix	kilo-	hecto-	deka-	(unit)	deci-	centi-	milli-
Symbol	k	h	da	(m, l, or g)	d	c	m
Decimal Meaning	1,000	100	10	1	1	.01	.001

THE METRIC UNITS AT A GLANCE

LENGTH
10 millimeters (mm) = 1 centimeter
10 centimeters (cm) = 1 decimeter
100 centimeters = 1 meter (m)
10 decimeters (dm) = 1 meter
1000 meters (m) = 1 kilometer (km)

CAPACITY (Volume)
1000 milliliters (ml) = 1 liter (l)
1000 liters = 1 kiloliter (kl)
1 cubic centimeter (cm3) = 1 milliliter
1 cubic decimeter (dm3) = 1 liter

MASS (Weight)
1000 milligrams (mg) = 1 gram
1000 grams = 1 kilogram (kg)
1000 kilograms = 1 metric ton (t)
1 metric ton = 1 megagram (mg)

AREA
100 square millimeters (mm^2) = 1 square centimeter (cm^2)
100 square centimeters = 1 square decimeter (dm^2)
100 square decimeters = 1 square meter (m^2)

TEMPERATURE
0°C = (zero degrees Celsius)
        the freezing point of water
37°C = the normal body temperature
100°C = the boiling point of water

ENGLISH AND METRIC COMPARED

APPROXIMATE EQUIVALENTS

LENGTH
1 mm = .039 in.   1 in. = 25.4 mm
1 cm = .39 in.   1 in. = 2.54 cm
1 m = 1.09 yd.   1 ft. = .3 m
1 m = 3.28 ft.   1 yd. = .91 m
1 km = .62 mi.   1 mi. = 1.6 km

MASS (Weight)
1 g = .035 oz.   1 oz. = 28 g
1 kg = 2.2 lb.   1 lb. = .45 kg

CAPACITY (Liquid Measurement)
1 ml = .03 fl. oz.   1 fl. oz. = 29.57 ml
1 l = 2.11 pt.   1 pt. = .47 l
1 l = 1.06 qt.   1 qt. = .95 l

TEMPERATURE
0° Celsius = 32° Fahrenheit
0° Fahrenheit = -17.8° Celsius

Use what you've learned.

Use the information on the prefix chart on page 83 to complete this table.

Name of Unit	Symbol	Change to	Operation	Example
millimeter	MM	cm	÷ 10	40 mm = ...4.....cm
	cm	mm	x 10	2 cm = ...mm
meter	m		x 100	3 m = ...cm
meter	m	km	÷ 1000	5000 m = ...m
kilometer		m		60 km = ...m
kilogram		g	x 1000	5 kg = ...g
gram			÷ 1000	2000 g = ...kg
	mg	g	÷ 1000	4000 mg = ...g
	g	mg		3 g = ...mg
liter		kl	÷1000	1200 l = ...kl
	ml		÷1000	4500 ml =...............l
kiloliter		l		3 kl = ...l

Due to space limitations, the answers to these questions do not appear in the answer key.

Using the units above, answer the following questions.

1. Which unit is often used to measure fabric? _____

2. Which unit is used to measure distances between cities? _____

3. Gasoline might be measured in _____.

4. The measurement of a large plot of land might be expressed in square _____.

5. A dime is about one _____ thick.

6. To find out how heavy a bag is, which unit would you use? _____

7. A dose of liquid medicine might be expressed in _____.

8. The net weight of a box of cereal might be expressed in _____.

9. Oven heat is expressed in _____.

10. The size of a tile is often expressed in _____.

Apply the comparisons to the following questions.

11. Which is thicker? 3 in. or 5 cm?_____

12. Is a 4 lb. package heavier than 2 kg? _____

13. Which is the larger container? 2 qt. or 2 l? _____

14. Is 65 km per hour within the 55 mph speed limit? _____

15. What is the metric height of a person who is 5 ft. tall? _____

16. Which is lighter? 9 oz. or 230 g? _____

17. Which cherries cost less? 10 lb. for $15 or 9 kg for $20? _____

18. Which temperature is warmer? 20° Celsius or 32° Fahrenheit? _____

19. Is a 62 in. bag larger or smaller than 145 cm? _____

20. You used to weigh 100 lb. Now you weigh 49 kg. Did you lose or gain weight? _____

5. Shopping With Foreign Money

Quick Reference

$ To change U.S. dollars into foreign currency X: Multiply the amount of U.S. dollars by the number of X in 1 U.S. dollar.

$ To change foreign currency X into U.S. dollars:

1. Divide the total amount of X by the number of X in 1 U.S. dollar.
2. Round your answer to the nearest cent.

A "perfect gift" from Germany costs only 66 marks! But is it **worth the price?** This lesson will show you how to convert from one country's money (currency) to another.

Canada	1.50 Canadian dollars = 1 U.S. dollar
France	7.08 francs = 1 U.S. dollar
Britain	.67 pound = 1 U.S. dollar
Japan	118 yen = 1 U.S. dollar
Germany	2.11 marks = 1 U.S. dollar

The equivalent value of one country's money to another changes from day to day. The conversions given in this lesson may not be valid at the time you actually shop abroad. Use them only to do questions 1–6 on page 86. When you need to know the current value of 1 U.S. dollar in foreign currency, check with your bank or in the travel section of the newspaper.

On Your Own

Make up a shopping list for a country you would like to visit. Find out from a bank how much 1 U.S. dollar is worth in that country's currency.

Item	Cost in Foreign Currency	Cost in U.S. Dollars

1. Upon arrival in each of the countries listed below, you immediately change 500 U.S. dollars to the local currency. How much do you have in each currency?

   Japan: ....*65,000*.........yen

   France: ....francs

   Germany: ....marks

   Britain: ....pounds

   Canada: ....Canadian dollars

   $$\begin{array}{r} 500 \\ \times\ 130 \\ \hline 65{,}000 \end{array}$$

2. You are sending a bottle of perfume to a friend in Japan. It cost you 24 U.S. dollars. How much is it in yen?

   _____

3. Your friend in Germany has asked you to buy a tennis racket that costs 35 U.S. dollars. How many marks should your friend send?

   _____

4. You wish to buy a radio in Japan that sells for 2795 yen. How much is it in U.S. dollars?

   _____

5. A wonderful French dinner costs you 75 francs. How many U.S. dollars are you spending?

   _____

6. The rain in England forced you to buy an umbrella for 8 pounds. How much is it in U.S. dollars?

   _____

1. Fill in the Pct. column to determine the standing of each team. Round your answers to three decimal places.

Team	W	L	Pct.
A's	76	86	_____
Braves	69	92	_____
Cardinals	95	67	_____
Cubs	76	85	_____
Dodgers	73	89	_____
Expos	91	71	_____
Yankees	90	72	_____
Mets	92	70	_____
Padres	65	97	_____
Pirates	80	82	_____

2. Fill in the missing distance, travel time, or average speed on this travel record.

Distance	Travel Time	Average Speed
250 mi.		50 mph
	$3\frac{1}{2}$ hr.	88 km/h
640 km	8 hr	
15 mi.		30 mph
760 km	$9\frac{1}{2}$ hr.	
	$\frac{1}{4}$ hr.	40 mph

Due to space limitations, this answer does not appear in the answer key.

3. Fill in the missing temperatures on this chart. Round your answers to one decimal place.

Degrees Fahrenheit	Degrees Celsius
32	
	37
45	
	21
90	
	19
75	
	40

Use this table to answer questions 4–6.

Italy 2089 lira = 1 U.S. dollar
Kenya 58.16 shillings = 1 U.S. dollar
Mexico 8.85 pesos = 1 U.S. dollar

(Remember, these rates change from day to day.)

4. If you change 50 U.S. dollars into the currency of each of these countries, how much will it be worth in local currency?

Italy: _____

Kenya: _____

Mexico: _____

5. An Italian hat sells for 73,115 lira. How much is this in U.S. dollars?

_____

6. A Mexican serape is priced at 120 pesos. How much is this in U.S. dollars?

_____

87

Skills Survey

Add the scores in questions 1–4. Then find the average of each score by dividing each sum by the number of scores added to get the sum. Round each answer to the nearest whole number.

1. 5
6
4)‾‾‾‾‾
3
2
6
+4

2. 34
46
36)‾‾‾‾‾
42
27
+13

3. 125
180
155)‾‾‾‾‾
200
+160

4. 95
110
124)‾‾‾‾‾
87
106
100
+98

Arrange the numbers in questions 5–7 from greatest to least in value.

5.
1.00	_____
.02	_____
3.20	_____
.12	_____
4.09	_____
4.25	_____
3.40	_____
1.60	_____
.50	_____

6.
.600	_____
.537	_____
.421	_____
.708	_____
.375	_____
.675	_____
.500	_____
.357	_____
.676	_____

7.
1.009	_____
.958	_____
1.010	_____
.957	_____
1.101	_____
.897	_____
1.001	_____
1.210	_____
.960	_____

Circle the operations you need to use for each problem in questions 8–10. (Hint: Sometimes there will be more than one answer.)

8. If a TD is 6 points, what is the total score for 6 TDs?

ADD   SUBTRACT   MULTIPLY   DIVIDE

9. What is your bowling average if you score 120, 130, and 110 in three games?

ADD   SUBTRACT   MULTIPLY   DIVIDE

10. In 29 games, the Eagles won 29. How many games did they lose?

ADD   SUBTRACT   MULTIPLY   DIVIDE

On Your Own

The time of day varies in different parts of the world. If it's 7:00 a.m. in New York, what time is it in Singapore, Paris, London, Madrid, Israel, Hawaii, and San Francisco? Use a time zone map in an almanac or encyclopedia to find out.

Use the following formula to solve problems 11 and 12: Distance = Speed x Time

11. In 5 hours, you were able to drive 250 miles. How fast were you going?

_____

12. You drove 100 kilometers at 50 kilometers per hour. How long did it take you?

_____

These are the meanings of important terms, as used in the context of this book.

Account—the record of one's money in a bank.

Addends—numbers to be added.

Addition—the operation of combining numbers to get a sum.

Area—the number of unit squares on a surface (length multiplied by width).

Area code—a number that identifies each telephone service area in a country.

Average—a number equal to the sum divided by the number of addends.

Balance—the amount of money remaining in an account after a deposit has been added or a payment has been subtracted.

Balance brought forward—the last balance on the previous page written on the first line of a new page.

Benefits (insurance)—the payments or services given by an insurance company as stated in a policy.

Bookkeeping—the method of recording the income and expenses of a business.

Budgeting—putting aside money for particular expenses.

Calculator—a machine used to compute math problems.

Cash—money that is immediately available to spend.

Cash record—a statement that shows the balance after adding amounts received or subtracting amounts paid out.

Celsius—the metric system's term used to express temperature.

Change—the coins or bills you get back after giving more money than what is due from you.

Check—a written order telling the bank to pay money from your account as instructed.

Check register—a record of deposits and checks written.

Commission—a percentage of a salesperson's total sales.

Commuters—regular riders.

Compute—to figure out the answer to a math problem.

Cost of goods sold—the amount paid by the seller for the things he or she sells.

Credit—a loan or borrowed amount to be paid back after the promised period of time.

Currency—money (coins or bills) that is used in exchange for goods or services.

Customer—someone who buys goods or services.

Debit—the amount of money subtracted from an account.

Decimal—a special type of fraction based on tenths.

Deductible (insurance)—initial specified amount to be paid by the insured; anything in excess of that amount will be paid by the insurance company.

Deductions—taxes and contributions subtracted from gross pay to get the net pay.

Denominator—the number of parts into which a whole has been divided; the number at the bottom of a fraction.

Deposit—to put money in a bank account.

Difference—the answer to a subtraction problem.

Digit—the figures 0, 1, 2, 3, 4, 5, 6, 7, 8, and 9 that make up numerals.

Discount—the amount taken off from the usual price.

Distance—the space between two points.

Division—the process of separating a whole amount of something into a number of parts.

Downpayment—a part of the full price paid at the time of purchase.

Expense—an amount paid out.

Fahrenheit—a term used to tell temperature.

FICA—Federal Insurance Contribution Act or Social Security tax.

Finance charge—interest or amount paid in addition to the amount borrowed.

Fixed expenses—amounts to pay that are the same or nearly the same each month.

Flexible expenses—amounts to pay that may vary, or are not needed each month.

Fraction—a part of a whole expressed as a number with a numerator and a denominator.

FWT—Federal Withholding Tax, or amount of federal income tax deducted from a paycheck.

Gross pay (income)—the total amount earned before any deductions are subtracted.

Gross profit—the total amount of money earned by a business before expenses are deducted.

Income—the amount of money earned from labor or from profit.

Income tax—the tax paid on an individual's (or business's) net income.

Insurance—coverage by contract for money losses in the case of fire, death, injury, or accidents.

Interest (simple)—a percent paid on an amount of money borrowed or a percent earned on an amount deposited in a savings account.

Glossary (cont.)

Installment—one of a series of payments made until the amount borrowed is completely paid for.

Kilo—the metric system's prefix that means one thousand; often used to mean kilogram.

Line graph—a pictorial representation of the rises and falls of a line formed by connected dots.

Loan—money lent with interest to a borrower for temporary use.

Long distance—telephone call made between two different area codes.

Mail—letters and packages sent from one place to another at the cost specified by the post office.

Mark-up—an amount added to the unit cost in order to find the selling price.

Meter—the basic unit of length in the metric system.

Mileage (MPG)—total miles traveled on one gallon of gasoline.

Multiplication—the process of adding a number to itself a specified number of times.

Net earning, income, or pay—the amount the individual takes home after all deductions have been made.

Net loss—amount of money lost when operating costs exceed profits.

New balance—in a record, the balance that appears after an expense has been recorded and subtracted.

Operating expenses—the amount of money needed to produce goods or services (rent, utilities, supplies, ads, and others).

Overtime—time in excess of a standard work day or schedule.

Paycheck—a written order telling the bank to pay the amount of salary earned by the person named.

Pct.—the abbreviation used in team standings for percent of games won in relation to the number of games played.

Percent—one part of a hundred.

Piece rate—amount of money earned for each piece made or sold.

Piecework earnings—income computed by multiplying piece rate times the number of pieces made or sold.

Place value—the value based on the location of a digit in a numeral.

Policy—the written agreement between the insured and the insurance company.

Postage—the fee paid for stamps needed to send a letter or package.

Pound (lb.)—a unit of mass or weight; equal to 16 ounces.

Premium—the amount paid to the insurance company for benefits promised.

Profit—amount of money retained after all expenses have been deducted.

Product—the answer to a multiplication problem.

Quantity (qty.)—number of items bought or sold.

Quotient—the answer to a division problem.

Ratio—the comparison of two amounts, usually named by a fraction.

Road map—a guide to the roads within a specified area.

Route—a fixed course of travel.

Salary—amount earned in exchange for labor.

Sale—selling of goods at discounted prices.

Sales report—a record of the total income of a business over a given period.

Sales tax—additional amount charged on goods and services based on a percentage of the purchase price; it is usually imposed by both state and city.

Savings account—a bank account in which money is deposited for safekeeping and for earning interest.

Schedule—a chart showing a timetable or transportation fares.

Speed—the rate at which a given distance is traveled.

Subtotal—a partial sum; the sum before a sales tax is added.

Subtraction—the process of finding the difference between two numbers.

Sum—the result of adding two numbers.

Table—information arranged in rows and columns for easy reference.

Tax—an amount of money charged by the government on products, services, property, or income.

Team standings—how teams rank based on the ratio of games won to the number of games played.

Temperature—a measure of how hot or cold the climate is.

Time—a period expressed in terms of seconds, minutes, hours, days, months, or years.

Time-and-a-half—a rate paid for overtime work usually equal to regular hourly rate X $1\frac{1}{2}$.

Total—the sum or product of a list of amounts.

Unit cost—the actual amount paid by the seller for one item for sale; such amounts are usually marked up for profit.

Utilities—gas, electricity, water, or other essentials in a home.

W-2 form—a statement of income and tax withheld.

Wholesale—the selling of large quantities of goods for resale by another person or business.

Withdraw—to take money out of a bank account.

Section 1: Just The Facts

Pages 9–10
Addition: Working Right to Left
1. a. 8   2. a. 8   3. a. 5
   b. 6   b. 3   b. 5
   c. 3   c. 9   c. 3
4. 368   5. 938   6. 0355

Addition: Working With More Than Two Numbers
1. 8   2. 13   3. 12
4. 20   5. 26

Addition: Regrouping
1. 90   9. 203   17. 1000
2. 95   10. 413   18. 1111
3. 81   11. 650   19. 1222
4. 97   12. 651   20. 1233
5. 114   13. 185   21. 2694
6. 160   14. 938   22. 3173
7. 117   15. 1174 23. 10,000
8. 123   16. 1245 24. 11,621

Lining Up Numbers to Add
1.   235   2.   4312
         4   34
        61   5
      4000   789
      4300   5140

Adding Long Columns
1. 2220   2. 2220
3. 2073   4. 2440

Page 12
Find the Difference
1. 18-9=7   2. 28-22=6
3. 39-7=32   4. 347-35=312
5. 635-213=422   6. 705-701=4

Remains and Regrouping
1. 19   8. 179   15. 87
2. 27   9. 589   16. 277
3. 19   10. 188   17. 5001
4. 38   11. 53   18. 1429
5. 49   12. 67   19. 489
6. 368   13. 88   20. 2678
7. 278   14. 89

Pages 14–15
Multiplication: Working From Right to Left
1. 69   2. 385
3. 602   4. 288
5. 560   6. 3066
7. 3208   8. 2793

Using Your Memory in Multiplication
1. 570   2. 435
3. 512   4. 274
5. 836   6. 3598

Using Two Partial Products
1. 966   2. 1426
3. 1539   4. 3168
5. 21,735 6. 38,816

Using Three Partial Products
1. 161,415   2. 42,804
3. 274,248   4. 162,397

Zeros in Multiplication
1. 72,160   2. 260,928
3. 101,706   4. 285,324

Multiplying by 10, 100, 1000
1. 580   2. 5800
3. 58,000 4. 6000
5. 450   6. 99,000
7. 12,500

Pages 17–18
Solving Division Problems
Find the Quotients
1. 92   2. 13

Zeros in the Quotient
Find the Quotients
1. 206   2. 305
3. 404   4. 502

Short Method of Dividing Round Numbers
Find the Quotients
1. 3   2. 5   3. 5   4. 4

What will be the first digit in each quotient?
1. a. 4   b. 3
2. a. 5   b. 5
3. a. 5   b. 4

Using Remainders in Division
Find the quotients and the remainders
1. 3 hours 18 minutes
2. 4 feet 8 inches
3. 3 days 14 hours
4. 34 pounds 12 ounces

Estimating
Pages 19–20
1. How much does each cassette cost? About $2
2. Can you buy 2 cassettes for $4? Yes
3. How many cassettes can $12 buy? 6

Use what you've learned.
Estimate the sums:
1. 800 + 700 = 1500
2. 3000 + 2000 = 5000
3. 60 + 80 + 40 = 180

Estimate the differences:
1. 700 - 600 = 100
2. 500 - 200 = 300
3. 6000 - 4000 = 2000

Estimate the products:
1. 30 x 30 = 900
2. 90 x 50 = 4500
3. 400 x 200 = 80,000

Estimate the quotients:
1. 4000 ÷ 80 = 50
2. 3000 ÷ 50 = 60

Page 22
Use what you've learned.
1. a   2. b   3. d
4. a. +   b. -   c. x   d. ÷
5. a. done for you
   b. AC 17 - 11 =
   c. AC 49 ÷ 7 =
   d. AC 36 x 12 =
   e. AC 3 + 7 + 9 - 8 =
   f. AC 17 - 6 + 11 - 2 =

Answer Key

Skills Survey

1. 97
2. 378
3. 978
4. 6177
5. 41
6. 73
7. 704
8. 1110

9.
```
    42
   200
  2312
     3
  2557
```

10.
```
     4
  7201
    33
   120
  7358
```

11. 31
12. 267
13. 5866
14. 2577
15. 96
16. 1204
17. 300
18. 2884
19. 768
20. 6578
21. 113,103
22. 152,608
23. 12
24. 97
25. 304
26. 50

Section 2: Your Daily Math
Page 28
Use what you've learned.

2.
```
  $3.95
  $3.75
  $3.79
Total $11.49
```

3.
```
  $3.95
  $1.00
Total  $4.95
```

4.
```
  $5.85
  $1.55
Total  $7.40
```

5.
```
  $4.50
  $1.00
  $1.65
Total  $7.15
```

6.
```
  $7.50
  $1.10
Total  $8.60
```

7.
```
  $3.75
  $3.75
  $3.79
Total $11.29
```

8.
```
  $4.25
  $1.35
  $1.55
Total  $7.15
```

9.
```
  $8.25
  $2.55
  $3.85
  $ .75
Total $15.40
```

10.
```
  $7.25
  $1.90
  $3.65
Total $12.80
```

11.
```
  $7.75
  $1.00
  $1.60
  $1.55
Total $11.90
```

Page 29
How to Save on Transportation

2. a. $7.75
   b. 10
   c. $50
   d. $5
   e. 40
   f. $160
   g. $4
   h. monthly

3. a. $10.50
   b. $3.86
   c. $6.64

Page 30
At the Grocery

2.
```
  $4.00
  $3.29
  $ .99
Total  $8.28
```

3.
```
  $6.29
  $2.63
  $3.83
Total $12.75
```

4.
```
  $ .50
  $1.55
  $3.29
  $1.05
Total  $6.39
```

5.
```
  $3.10
  $2.99
  $4.72
  $2.33
Total $13.14
```

Page 32
Putting It All Together

1. $18.75

2. Monday's end balance: $71.50
   Tuesday's end balance: $64.62
   Wednesday's end balance: $31.93
   Thursday's end balance: $14.59
   Friday's end balance: $4.34
   End-of-week balance: $4.34

3. $9.90

4. Toronto $.75, New York City $.75, San Francisco $.73, Houston $.74

5. a. monthly b. regular one-way

6. =$11.03, =$9.80, = $7.35, =$4.90, =$3.68

7. a. initial 3 minutes = $2.85
   additional 7 min. = 2.03
   total cost = $4.88

   b. initial 1 minute = $.40
   add 9 minutes = $1.08
   total $1.48
   The difference in cost is $3.40.

Page 33
Skills Survey

1. 219
2. 3868
3. $39.69
4. $181.29
5. $29.94
6. 4114
7. 76
8. $4.10
9. $16.04
10. $96.09
11. 137,150
12. 68,320
13. 2.61
14. 3.2615
15. 1.0875
16. 424
17. 124
18. 2.15
19. 1.5
20. 2.65
21. .15
22. .44
23. 12.26
24. 2.29
25. 2.12
26. 10
27. 36.91
28. 9.48
29. 6.48
30. 6.26
31. 126.82
32. 168.22

Page 35–36
Use what you've learned.

1.

DEPOSIT SLIP
Nickel Bank and Trust Co.

Name **Your Name**

Date **1/1/1**

Checking

Account # **00-00-0**

		Dollars	Cents
	Cash	30	52
Checks	1	40	50
	2	14	15
	3		
Bank Use only	Total	85	17

2.

DEPOSIT SLIP

Date **1/11/1**

Checking Account # **00-00-0**

Name **Your Name**

		Dollars	Cents
	Cash	35	75
Checks	1	5	98
	2	15	00
	3	76	83
	4		
	5		
Bank Use only	Total	133	56

3.

No. 292

Sept. 5 20 *01*

Pay to the order of *Grand Sound* $ *89.95*

Eighty-nine and 95/100 Dollars

United Money Bank
Main Street

memo *Your Signature*

:027::091:447259:292

4.

No. 293

Oct. 7 20 *01*

Pay to the order of *Fine Jewel Co.* $ *183.97*

One hundred eighty-three and 97/100 Dollars

United Money Bank
Main Street

memo *Your Signature*

:027::091:447259:293

5.

No. 293

Nov. 10 20 *01*

Pay to the order of *Cash* $ *25.00*

Twenty-five 00/100 Dollars

United Money Bank
Main Street

memo *Your Signature*

:027::091:447259:294

Page 39
Savings
1. 5%
2. a. $3.42
   b. $4.67

Section 3: Your Money and Math
Page 40
Use what you've learned.
1. a. $.80   b. $64.80   c. $.81

Page 41
Budgeting
Flexible expenses: Answers will vary.

page 42
Use what you've learned.
Net Monthly Income $660

Fixed Expenses:

Rent $255

Telephone $29.50

Car Payment. $68.13

Gas & Repairs. $40

Electricity $12.37

Total Fixed Expenses . . . $405

Balance. $255

Flexible expenses: Answers will vary, but sum should not exceed $175.

Page 44
Use what you've learned.
Paycheck is $1,256 monthly, rent/transportation budget is $439.60.

Actual Costs	A	B
Rent	$400	$400
Utilities	0	$25
Transportation	$60	0
Total Monthly Cost	$460	$425

Can Jim pay the total monthly cost for each apartment? No

Which apartment should he rent? Apartment B

Pages 46–47
All About Credit
2. DVD player

   Total amt. of payments $330

   Less cash price $270.95

   Cost of credit $59.05

3. Desktop computer

   Total amt of payments $1,440

   Less cash price $1,100

   Cost of credit $340

Answer Key

Loans

4. Which of these loans has the lowest rate of interest? a.
   a. rate= .01 or 1%
   b. rate= .02 or 2%
   c. rate=.012 or 1.2%
5. $1.20
6. $46.69
7. $120
Interest added next month: $1.80.

Pages 50–51
Putting It All Together

4. $3
5. $900
Net monthly expenses: $900.

Fixed expenses:
Rent $275
Loan payment ...$45
Utilities $25
Telephone $12
Total Fixed Exp. .$357
Balance $543
Flexible expenses: Answers will vary.
6. A
7. $1,300, $1,040, $260
8. $6.05

Page 52
Skills Survey

1. a. six and 00/100
   b. one hundred one and 50/100
   c. fifty-eight and 34/100
   d. one thousand two hundred and 00/100
2. a. $483.12
   b. $1420.75
3. Jan. 1 $1,170.75
   Jan. 15 $1,095.25
   Jan. 18 $697
4. a. $2,700
   b. $817.56
   c. $2,044.20
5. a. $.02 or 2%
   b. $.01 or 1%
6. a. $66
   b. $258.75

Section 4: Math Goes to Work
Page 54
The Best Paying Job

2. Fast Food Cashier Trainee

Gross pay	$130
Total deductions	$40.82
Net pay	$89.18

3. Travel Guide

Gross pay	$220
Total deductions	$69.08
Net pay	$150.92

Page 55
Working Time

Total time Johnson:
20 hr. 25 min.

Total time Angeles:
20 hr. 45 min.

Total time Brown:
22 hr. 40 min.

Total time Sherman:
32 hr. 40 min.

Total time Cheng:
37 hr. 30 min.

Total time Perez:
40 hr. 30 min.

Page 57
Use what you've learned.

A. Regular pay =
   $8.50 x 35 = $297.50
B. Overtime =
   39.5 - 35 = 4.5
C. Time-and-a-half=
   $8.50 x 1.5 = $12.75
D. Overtime pay =
   $12.75 x 4.5 = $57.38
E. Gross earnings =
   $97.50 + $57.38 = $354.88

Page 58
Earning by Piece or Commission

1. $1.39 x 95 = $132.05
2. Piece rate for small belts = $.50
   Earnings = $12.50

   Piece rate for medium belts = $.75
   Earnings = $21.75

   Piece rate for large belts = $1.00
   Earnings = $27.00

   Total belts made = 81 Total Earnings =
   $61.25
3. Commission = 5% of $145,000 =
   .05 x 145,000 = $7,250
4. What percent commission are you
   being paid? = .08 x 100 = 8%

Page 59
What Is Profit? Loss?

1. $2.50
2. Cost of plain T-shirt $3.99
   Additional cost of letters
   + $2.50
   Cost of T-shirt $6.49
   Profit +$4.00
   Selling Price $10.49
3. Cost of T-shirt for Sale
                      $6.49
   Amount paid to you $5
   Difference $1.49
   Is this a profit or loss? Loss.

Page 60
Use what you've learned.

A. total sales $712.50
B. 1500 x .05 = $75
D. $275
E. 2000 x .05 = $100
F. $175   G. $537.50
I. $395   J. $142.50

Page 61
Pricing

1. Mark-up = $2.50 x 400%
            = $2.50 x 4
            = $10
   Selling Price = $.2.50 + $10
                 = $12.50

2.

% Mark-up	Mark-up	Total Mark-up or Gross Profit
20%	$2.40	$480
25%	$3	$525
30%	$3.60	$360
35%	$4.20	$210

The mark-up with the highest gross profit: 25%.

Page 62
Bookkeeping

1.
June 5 balance	$335.60
June 5 balance	$837.55
June 12 balance	$1,587.55
June 14 balance	$1,564.75
June 15 balance	$1,314.75
June 19 balance	$1,935.25

2.
June 5 total	$302.95
June 12 total	$550
June 19 total	$620.50
June 26 total	$844.30
Sweaters total	$1184
Vests total	$627.90
Blouses	$505.85
Total	$2,317.75

3. Total amount paid $715.90
   Total sweaters $ 287.50
   Total vests $178.95
   Total blouses $249.45

4. Total amount paid $456.30
   Total spent on ads $110.00
   Total spent on phone, etc
                        $265.40
   Total spent on supplies $55.40
   Total spent on other $25.50

Pages 63–64
Putting It All Together

1. Gross pay $556.50
   Total deductions $126.24
   Net pay $430.26

2. 1 wk. total   14 hr. 15 min.
   Actual time   12 hr. 30 min.
   Total in 4 weeks 50 hr. 00 min.
   Stella's average? 6 hr. 15 min.

3. A. 7   B. $9
   C. $210   D. $63
   E. $273

4. a $2.50   b $23.94

5. a. $10   b. $6

Page 65
Skills Survey

1. a. 24.63, b. 4 hr. 25 min.,
   c. 9 hr. 15 min., d. 49.99

2. a. $1233.20, b. $677.33,
   c.2 hr 5 min., d. 45 min.,
   e. $145.58

3. a. $542.50, b. .875, c. 9 hr. 30 min.,
   d. 9 hr. 30 min., e.18 hr. 20 min.

4. a. 2.08, b. .2, c. 3 hr. 2 min.,
   d. 1 hr. 36 min., e. .02

5. a. $15.00, b. 27.00, c. $46,
   d. $1.26, e., $.07, f. $.35

Section 5: Math Savers
Page 68

1. a. city = 2.78, highway = 7.69,
   total gallons used = 10.47

   b. city = 2.63, highway = 8,
   total gallons used = 10.63

   c. city = 2.94, highway = 7.14,
   total gallons used = 10.08

2. a. city = 11.11, highway = 1.92,
   total gallons used = 13.03

   b. city = 10.53, highway = 2,
   total gallons used = 12.53

   c. city = 11.76, highway = 1.79,
   total gallons used = 13.55

3. a. city = 5, highway = 8.06,
   total gas in one week = 13.06,
   weekly cost = $20.24

   b. city = 6, highway = 10.42,
   total gas in one week = 16.42,
   weekly cost = $25.45

   c. city = 7.06, highway = 10.87,
   total gas in one week = 17.93,
   weekly cost = $27.79

   d. city = 8, highway = 13.16,
   total gas in one week = 21.16,
   weekly cost = 32.80

Page 69
Gas-Saving Habits

1. a. 10   b.15
2. 22.5
3. 15
4.

MPH	Number of Gallons Used	Total Cost of Gasoline
30	4	$6.40
50	5	$8.00
80	7.5	$12.00

5. 2, 30
6. $321.25

Page 74
Buy More, Pay Less

1. $.02
2. $.20
3. a. $4.90
   b. $4.55
   c. $4.30
   d. $.92
   e. $.57
   f. $.32
4. Yes
5. a. $6.03
   b.the kit
   c. the kit

Page 75
Putting It All Together

1.

	Saab	Honda	Kia
City MPG	17	18	19
Highway MPG	22	26	27
City Gasoline	1.8	1.7	1.6
Highway Gasoline	1.8	1.5	1.5
Total	3.6	3.2	3.1

2. $4.50
3. 24 mpg
4. 16 mpg
5. living room 49 sq. yd.
   dining area 16 sq. yd.
   kitchen 6 sq. yd.
6. Jim's discount: $59.24
   Jim's sale price: $120.26
   Pat's discount: $40.70
   Pat's sale price: $122.10
   Len's discount: $29.99
   Len's sale price: $119.96
7. a. $.77
   b. $.90
   c. $7.90

Page 76
Skills Survey

1. Beetle 36, Camry 61, Range Rover 55,
   Saturn 50
2. a. 11 yd., b. 15 yd.,
   c. 19 yd.
3. a 216 in., b. 144 in.,
   c. 252 in.
4. a. 8 ft., b. 12 ft., c. 23 ft.
5. a. 108 sq. ft., b. 10 m2,
   c. 2688 sq in.
6. a $11.34, b. $25.91,
   c. $37
7. $.63
8. 2 for $.99
9. $.07

Answer Key

Section 6: Math Where You Least Expect It

Page 78
Where Does Your Team Stand?
1. Portland
2. Indiana
3. Milwaukee
4. Nets
5. a. Portland
   b. Phoenix
   c. Seattle
   d. Golden State
   e. Los Angeles

Page 79–80
Use what you've learned.
1. Southeast
2. Route 295
3. 58 km/hr
4. 100 km
5. 76 km/hr
6. 20 mph
7. Route 193

Page 82
Use what you've learned.

1. Anchorage   0C
   Miami   25C
   Phoenix   30C
   Seattle   5C
   Wichita   15C

2. Athens   59F
   Bangkok   95F
   Copenhagen   41F
   Peking   52F
   Rome   64F
3. No
4. Yes
5. Montreal
6. Chicago
7. -5°F
8. -5°C

Page 84
1. meter
2. kilometer
3. liter
4. meters
5. millimeter
6. kilogram
7. milligrams
8. grams
9. degrees Celsius
10. square centimeters
11. 3 in.

12. No
13. 2 liters
14. Yes
15. 1.5 meters
16. 230 g
17. 9 kg for $20
18. 20 Celsius
19. Larger
20. Gain

Page 86
Use what you've learned.

1. Japan   59,000 yen
   France   3,540 francs
   Germany   1,055 marks
   Britain   335 pounds
   Canada   750 Canadian pounds

2. 2832 yen
3. 73,85 marks
4. $23.69
5. 10.59 francs
6. $11.94

Page 87
Putting It All Together
Astros   .469
Braves   .429
Cardinals   .586
Cubs   .472
Dodgers   .451
Expos   .562
Yankees   .556
Mets   .568
Padres   .401
Pirates   .494

3. 32 F   =   0 C
   98.6 F =   37 C
   45 F   =   7.2 C
   69.8 F =   21 C
   90 F   =   32.2 C
   66.2 F =   19 C
   75 F   =   23.9 C
   104 F   =   40 C

4. Italy: 104,450 lira
   Kenya: 2908 shillings
   Mexico: 442.50 pesos
5. $35
6. $13.56

Page 88
Skills Survey
1. 30, 4
2. 197, 33
3. 820, 164
4. 720, 103
5. 4.25, 4.09, 3.40, 3.20, 1.60, 1.00, .50, .12, .02
6. .708, .676, .675, .600, .537, .500, .421, .375, .357
7. 1.210, 1.101, 1.010, 1.009, 1.001, .960, .958, .957, .897
8. Multiply
9. Add, Divide
10. Subtract
11. 50 mph
12. 2 hrs.